ONE WITHOUT THE OTHER

Stories of Unity Through Diversity and Inclusion

Shelley Moore
Foreword by Leyton Schnellert

PORTAGE &
MAIN PRESS

For Lorne Bodin

© 2016 Shelley Moore (text)

Portage & Main Press gratefully acknowledges the financial support of the Province of Manitoba through the Department of Sport, Culture and Heritage and the Manitoba Book Publishing Tax Credit, and the Government of Canada through the Canada Book Fund (CBF) for our publishing activities.

Printed and bound in Canada by Friesens
Design and cover art by Relish New Brand Experience
Illustrations by Jess Dixon

LIBRARY AND ARCHIVES CANADA CATALOGUING IN PUBLICATION

Moore, Shelley, author
    One without the other : stories of unity through diversity
& inclusion / Shelley Moore.

ISBN 978-1-55379-658-9 (paperback)

    1. Inclusive education. I. Title.

LC1200.M665 2016   371.9'046   C2016-900408-2

Also issued in electronic format: ISBN 978-1-55379-699-2 (EPUB)
                                    ISBN 978-1-55379-700-5 (MOBI)

25 24 23 22   6 7 8 9 10

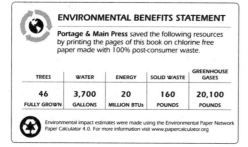

ENVIRONMENTAL BENEFITS STATEMENT

Portage & Main Press saved the following resources by printing the pages of this book on chlorine free paper made with 100% post-consumer waste.

TREES	WATER	ENERGY	SOLID WASTE	GREENHOUSE GASES
46	3,700	20	160	20,100
FULLY GROWN	GALLONS	MILLION BTUs	POUNDS	POUNDS

Environmental impact estimates were made using the Environmental Paper Network Paper Calculator 4.0. For more information visit www.papercalculator.org

FSC
www.fsc.org

MIX
Paper from
responsible sources
FSC® C016245

PORTAGE &
MAIN PRESS

www.portageandmainpress.com
Winnipeg, Manitoba
Treaty 1 Territory and homeland of the Métis Nation

Contents

Foreword

Why do we do what we do? What is the legacy we leave as educators? These are questions I've been wondering about lately. As an inclusive educator who is passionate about social justice and equity, teaching is not just a job. It's a passion. It's a vehicle to make a difference not just in the classroom, but in our communities and society. This book makes just such a contribution. Through story and metaphor, Shelley touches the heart and helps us to embrace diversity and move toward greater equity in our classrooms.

Educators need inspiration. We need new ways to consider and renew our practice. Shelley Moore's work provokes us. It illustrates how we can align our values and practice. It's hard to argue with the concept of inclusion. But what does it really mean? What can it look like? Shelley's work takes up concepts such as Universal Design for Learning (UDL). With "The Sweeper Van," Shelley helps us deepen our understanding of UDL. She's right. We all need increased support at different points in our lives. With humour and *gravitas,* Shelley shows that how and when these supports are put into place for some, they can benefit many.

With stories like "Presuming Competence," Shelley illustrates how students who provoke and challenge us offer us the opportunity to move into the unknown and develop our pedagogy. With this book, Shelley brings this point home time and time again.

Shelley was and is that student for me. She has helped me to see students as more than a *snapshot.* I've come to know Shelley through many lenses.

I was Shelley's teacher in grades 8 and 9 in Edmonton and then again during her Masters work at Simon Fraser University, and I now work with her as a PhD student. I also know her as a teacher and co-researcher and friend. As I taught and learned with Shelley over these past three decades, she has offered me many a "telling moment." Her questions, protestations, risk taking, and creativity have helped me to see teaching and learning in new ways. Her teaching, learning, and research extend the ideas I take up in my scholarship. This is why I do what I do. What is my legacy? It's seeing my student surpass what I could only dream. It's seeing the next generation of innovators like Shelley reimagine and recognize social justice and equity in profound new ways that change outcomes for students who are the *outside pins* and showing how inclusive classrooms can increase the learning and life chances of all students. Wrapped up in these stories and metaphors are practices and insights to provoke and inspire. This book documents the beginnings of Shelley's legacy.

Enjoy the metaphors, stories, perspectives, and learning that accompany *One Without the Other.*

Leyton Schnellert, PhD
Faculty of Education
University of British Columbia Okanagan

Introduction

I was teaching a course last summer at the University of British Columbia called "Conceptual Foundations of Inclusive Education." Thirty or so practising teachers from various subject areas, knowledge expertise, and experience levels from across British Columbia joined me for three weeks of deconstruction, inquiry, and reflection, creating an engaging community of learners. The course was in July, and on this particular day, it was my birthday. We started the class with some cupcakes and hung up "Happy Birthday" bunting across the whiteboard, before diving into our explorations and understanding of the concept driving learning systems all over the world – inclusive education.

I showed a slide to my students with four bubbles (see figure I.1, page 2). Their job was to label the bubbles with the appropriate terms (*inclusion, integration, exclusion,* and *segregation*) based on their own experiences and prior knowledge of the concepts.

After some discussion, it was agreed that Bubble C in fact represented inclusion (see figure I.2, page 3). This is the common consensus arrived at in many groups I have worked with, both in pre- and in-service professional development settings.

After some discussion, however, a student commented, "Shelley, I don't think this diagram is inclusion, either." This caught me off guard.

"Of course this is inclusion!" I thought. I had shown this slide to hundreds if not thousands of people! What could she possibly mean?

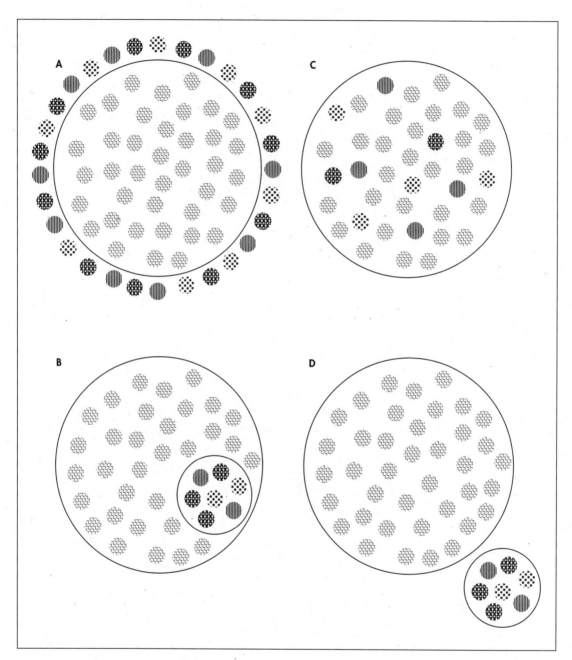

Figure I.1

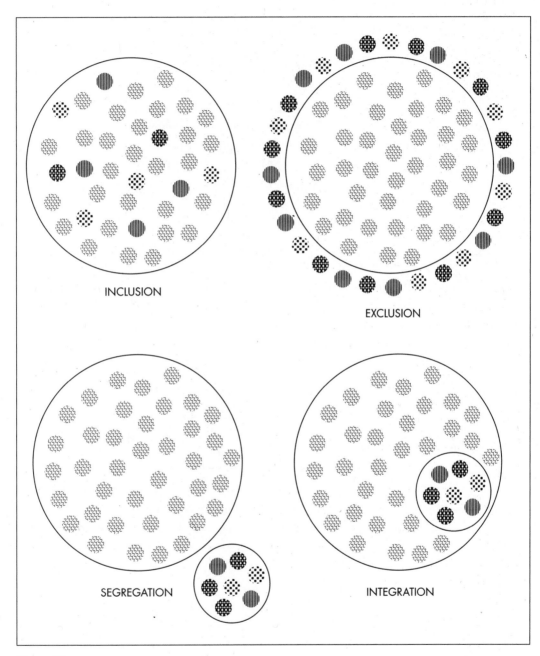

INCLUSION

EXCLUSION

SEGREGATION

INTEGRATION

Figure I.2

She explained, "Look what you have shown us. I see a bubble with a whole bunch of wavy dots. And then, there are a scattered handful of other patterned dots."

"Yeah," I said, "and…."

"Well, in my definition of inclusion, there is no *other*."

I stood there speechless, because she was absolutely right. The diagram I was presenting was not one of inclusion; it was an example of the traditional model of education. The model where our goal is to produce more of the same – lingering evidence of the factory model of education where we needed to produce and replicate people to meet the demand of the workforce during the industrial revolution (Robinson 2009; Zhao 2009). A model where our job as educators (and especially special educators) is to identify students who aren't wavy, and fix them. Send the checkered kids to the checkered teacher, the diamond kids to the diamond teacher, and the striped kids to the striped teacher. This model of education is a deficit, medical model, and I was showing the class a perfect example of how it was still plaguing us today. But more and more kids are coming to us not wavy! Not only is this model less effective, but also we are running out of funding, supports, and students to allow this model to continue. Some have met this shift in paradigm with panic; others are seeing it as an opportunity. This paradigm shift, however, is long overdue, and we need to start matching our goals of education to the goals and expectations needed to meet the current demands of our society – which no longer wants people to simply comply. This is especially true now, as more and more occupations involving compliance and replication are being replaced by machines (Zhao 2009).

Educational reforms are happening on a global scale, including in British Columbia and other provinces in Canada, where the Ministries of Education are completely restructuring their curricula, being designed and written by teachers for teachers, with the emphasis on moving away from classrooms of wavy students (BC Ministry of Education 2015). We are no longer living in the Industrial Revolution; this is the 21st century – where we need to value the strengths rather than deficits in learning. Rather than finding out why students aren't wavy, our job is now to find out what their pattern is. What do they bring? What can they contribute *because* of their diverse and unique expertise? For decades we have been trying to take this "pattern" out of our students, taking the special out of special education, the autistic out of autism, the language out of cultures, and, especially, the Indigenous out of First Nations, Métis, and Inuit children. This is not teaching to diversity. This is not inclusive. Teaching to diversity and inclusion is where we value the characteristics that *are* diverse, and not try and homogenize them.

The class continued to discuss what the conceptual diagram of inclusion could be, and together we decided that the only way to ensure there was no "other" was not to make us all wavy, but instead to make us all "an other" (see figure I.3).

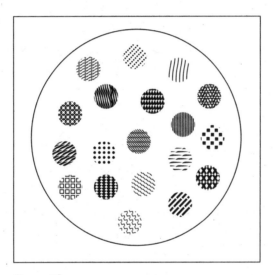

Figure I.3

When looking at inclusion this way, it also helped us realize that this is no longer an idea specific to special education. There is a distinct gap between the silos of special education and curriculum (Pugach and Warger 2001; Thomas and Loxley 2007), but if we look at inclusion as a concept of teaching to the diversity of all, rather than just a special-education initiative, we can bridge this gap. We are diverse, all of us. We all have strengths, we all have stretches, and we all need to get better at something. The difference in teaching to diversity, however, is that we don't start with our deficits; we start with our strengths, and this includes students, teachers, support staff, custodians, bus drivers, and parents. My good friend Leyton Schnellert refers to this collective as "the ecology of learning communities." Inclusive education relies on the diversity of its ecosystem to not only promote coexistence and tolerance, but to thrive on the learning and interaction of each person in the community

Through this discussion, I also realized that if we can now extend inclusive education to include every diverse learner, then we can also start to view inclusion as not something we simply do; instead, it becomes something that just *is*. We cannot escape or avoid the diversity in our world by attempting to homogenize and standardize our classrooms and learners. Homogeneity is a battle that has never been won and never will be. Civilizations have collapsed in their attempts to make everyone the same (Morris 2013). This is no longer our vision of education (thank goodness), and we are long overdue in matching our vision to our practices in classrooms, schools, and communities.

It was also on this particular day that I was inspired to write this book, because it was on this day I realized that if inclusion and diversity is something that just *is,* then it is also something we live, something we are, and something we believe in together. And it is through this common goal that we can also be unified: we can be *one* without being an *other*.

So, please allow me to introduce to you *"One* without the *Other."*

PART 1
What Is Inclusion? Debunking the Myths

You may be hard-pressed to find someone who doesn't believe in inclusion and the values of diversity on some level. Plus, it is pretty hard to avoid. Ken Robinson (2009) said it best: "The only thing students have in common is the year of their birth!" The individuals of the world are not packaged into neat little packages of people organized by age or ability, gender, or language (although I suppose there are some who would like to try!). Can you imagine if, when we walked into a grocery store, access to checkout tills were determined by these labels? It would be an absurd idea in every place in society, except in the classrooms of our schools. This unnatural arrangement is where the practical aspects of inclusion get messy, definitions of the concept start to get fuzzy, and our practices become a mismatch to our beliefs about what inclusion means in the world outside our classroom doors. It doesn't take long to notice how frequently we all, even if in the same school or community, understand inclusion differently.

Early in my career, I realized this discrepancy, and it caused tensions in my quest to understand inclusion in both philosophical and practical terms. My first question was: If we are to believe in and try to move forward in our inclusive practice as educators, don't we all need to have a common understanding of what it means? The unfortunate reality, however, is that the term *inclusion* has become contaminated (Thomas and Loxley 2007). A once-powerful word that drove equal access campaigns for students of different abilities, strengths, and challenges, the term *inclusion* has instead come to be associated with lack of funding, time, and supports – a political playing card that has turned our most vulnerable learners into a burden, defined by ratios and deficits. Further tension emerges when trying to create a consensus of how to enact practices of inclusion across districts, schools, and classrooms, leaving both teachers and students feeling like they are being shuffled around a building without the supports, resources, and understanding behind the inclusive rationale. The reality, however, is that there is no answer. There is no one way of being inclusive. Addressing diversity can be achieved in many ways, depending on the history, experience, knowledge, and philosophies of the stakeholders involved. Somewhere along this quest, however, answers have collided, and where once stood a common philosophy bringing educators together, myths and assumptions have formed about the practicalities of inclusive education that divide staff, parents, and students alike.

Reclaiming the word and concept of inclusive education and calibrating our definitions among teachers, administrators, support staff, parents, and students was the beginning of my inclusive journey, and so, I thought, what a perfect place to begin this text. What is inclusion – both philosophically *and* practically? And how can we align these definitions so that our practices better match our beliefs as individuals, schools, and communities of natural diversity? Part of this reclamation is to simply debunk some of the myths driving the education silos, but also to start to reconstruct the practical realities of inclusive education.

In the following chapters, I attempt to describe these practical implications of inclusive education to help situate the rest of this text and to connect our values of inclusion to our everyday practices.

Inclusion Is Not Just About Students with Special Needs

When I began teaching, my first position was in a co-taught grade 4/5 classroom. I was a special educator in a beautiful school in Bronx, N.Y., teaming up with an amazing local – who could both charm and straighten out kids (and me) in a fraction of a second with a simple glance in their (or my) direction. Given the context, the school was also placed with the unfair burden of trying to negotiate additional factors, such as poverty, hunger, crime, and the general health and well-being of students and families, who were struggling to exist in a world not built to support them. It was here, however, that I also found what loyalty, compassion, and family meant, in a forgotten neighbourhood that I will never forget. I forged friendships and learned lessons for a lifetime there, and will always be grateful for the welcome and belonging I felt in this wonderful community.

On finishing my undergraduate degree in special education, I was skeptical of inclusion. I couldn't help wondering if the learning of tolerance for the "other" kids was a strong enough reason for kids to be forced together, simply breathing the same air, at the expense of explicit instruction for students who needed it the most. "Inclusion for the sake of inclusion" is what I called it, and for me, it wasn't a good enough reason. Well, it took me two days of teaching in the Bronx for me to realize how my understanding of the practice of inclusive education was inaccurate. Inclusion wasn't about tolerance, it was about celebration! I learned the value of collaboration, multiple expertise, and the rich benefits of cultural diversity in an inclusive framework that I had previously and mistakenly understood as a framework supporting an expert model – where I thought I knew everything, and my job was to bestow my gifts of knowledge onto students and staff alike. This transmissive approach (Miller 2007) to learning did not get me far, and if I was to survive, I needed to adapt to inclusion, diversity, and collaboration quickly!

My two years in New York set me straight, as New York does, and when arriving back to Canada to complete my Masters, I had a new understanding of inclusive philosophy and the experience to back it up.

However, if New York taught me about the richness in diversity, McNair Secondary, my second teaching position, taught me about the beauty of acceptance. For the next seven years, I settled into this secondary school in Richmond, British Columbia, where I found my new home teaching students with developmental disabilities in grades 8–12. In New York, similar to many districts and schools, students with the most significant disabilities are still not included in classrooms with their peers, and are often sent to segregated schools, classrooms, or programs (Pugach and Warger 2001). Even in the literature and research, inclusive education practice and strategies are most visible when supporting students with high incidence disabilities, such as learning disabilities, high-functioning autism, at-risk behaviour, certain mental-health difficulties, and so on (Downing 2008; Katims 2000).

With a three-decade-strong inclusion philosophy, the Richmond School District prides itself on neighbourhood schools where students of all ability belong. From the ripe ages of three and four, students who traditionally have been segregated because of their ability, instead learn alongside their peers in classrooms. By the time they get to grade 8, all kids are part of cohorts that grow up together, go to birthday parties together, eat lunch together, and give each other high fives down the hallway. There are no "those kids" or "that classroom." Kids are kids, and I saw it every day in the halls of my new school. This was not tolerance – this was acceptance.

Inclusion means everyone – but *actually* everyone, even our students who need the most support in our classrooms, schools, and communities. If New York taught me about cultural and language diversity, Richmond taught me about the importance of the diversity of ability. But both places taught me that *all* diversities need to be considered and celebrated. Inclusion is not just about students with special needs, it is about *all* students, and before we can even begin to align philosophy with practice, and shift our deficit-based education paradigm to a strength-based model, we need to understand this essential condition.

Inclusion Is Not Integration

To understand what inclusion is, we also have to understand what it isn't. Part of the reason *inclusion* as a term has been contaminated is that it is used synonymously with the word *integration*. Likewise, although I have never stepped into a school whose mission statement values segregation and exclusion, I have seen, in many schools, students experiencing all of exclusion, segregation, integration, and inclusion depending on the day, time, teacher, support staff, subject area, and grade (see Introduction, figure I.1).

To understand these terms better, let's look back to periods in history that we associate these words with. What events come to mind, for example, when you read the words *integration* and *segregation?* Many may recall the civil rights movement of the 1960s, apartheid, residential schools for First Nations children, or the Nazi occupation of World War II. These are definitely not times associated with communities of learning and the celebration of diversity! What all these events have in common, however, is that they involved forced movement of groups of people – who had no choice. They were either separated or brought together, sharing space – breathing the same air.

Now, we don't have to go back in time to see this happening every day. On a much less traumatic scale, we can say that education systems in general are integration. We force kids to come to school every day. School buildings and classrooms are just containers holding different groups of people, and without facilitation and explicit attention of teaching skills, students and staff alike will naturally gravitate to contexts that are familiar and safe, whether arranged into groups by themselves or by others (Benard 1991; Gibbs 2006; Thomas and Loxley 2007). Just go to the nearest high school to see this phenomenon in our schools today. Just like when I went to high school, the athletic kids were in the gym, the drama kids were in the back of the school, the special-education kids were hidden down a hallway, the students who needed English language support were pulled out on Tuesday afternoons. The leadership kids had a room, the kids who smoked had a pit, and the front of our school was surrounded by kids who dressed like hikers, but didn't hike.

This is integration – groups of students housed together. There is no choice: go here, go there, don't go here, don't go there. At one point in the history of education, I can appreciate that this was a first big step toward inclusive education, but evolution has taught us this isn't enough. There has to be something else that happens in these buildings, or schools are just containers of integration (Thomas and Loxley 2007).

Continuing with this idea of containers, we can also compare segregation and exclusion, whereby segregation involves the separation of groups, and exclusion involves the separation of individuals. Students of diverse cultures, genders, languages, religions, and so on may experience segregation, whereas individuals with disabilities, people who are transgendered or identify as LGBTQ2S, or even kids like me who were a little plumper than their peers, are some examples of those who often experience exclusion.

If we understand segregation, integration, and exclusion as this idea of forced containers, there becomes a clear distinction between inclusion and the rest. Inclusion, unlike the other three, is the only one of the four that is a voluntary community. We can force people together and apart all we want, but we cannot force people to engage in a community.

I realized this subtle difference when I first jumped on the inclusion bandwagon as a teacher and tore through my secondary school, demanding inclusion in every classroom and student experience in the school. Although the students with developmental disabilities at the high school I worked at were included socially in many areas, it was still unclear what their role in their classes looked like, especially since their opportunities for inclusion were often limited to elective classes. So I was set on making sure they were included everywhere!

On a chilly Thursday afternoon in September, however, the school organized a pep rally for all the grades. I had never been to a pep rally, so the boat horn, banging pots and pans, gym filled with hundreds of screaming teenagers' sensory nightmare was new to me. But it wasn't about *me!* I was being inclusive! So, my 16 students with developmental disabilities and I walked down to the gym – to be inclusive! As we got closer, however, my trail of students lagged farther behind me, with looks of anxiety creeping onto their faces. I simply responded to this worry with, "Come on! There are headphones if it's too loud! We are being inclusive!"

I will never forget one little guy's face when he came up to me and finally said, "Ummm, Ms. Moore. You know that half of us have autism, right?"

What I failed to realize in my fit of inclusion, was that *forcing* them to go to the pep rally was as segregative as if I had *prevented* them from going in the first place. What *would* have been inclusive is if I had said, "Okay, everyone, the pep rally is today! There are headphones for your ears and chairs close to the door for quick escape, or you can just go and scream your face off! It is up to you!" The inclusivity came when I presented the *opportunity* for them to attend a school experience with *support.*

Including students in the pep rally had to be more meaningful that just forcing them to go. I had to also consider the purpose, and give them the choice of participating; otherwise, I was defeating the purpose of the goal I had set out to meet.

On the other side of that coin, however, is that sometimes we are quick to discount a setting, class, or experience for students based on similar assumptions, such as, "Oh, they won't like it," or, "What are those students going to get out of it?" Instead, we end up excluding kids rather than giving them these opportunities with support.

Take me, for example. I can present and speak to hundreds of people – no problem! Presenting is *so* easy for me – it is one of my strengths. No one ever believes me when I tell them that I am an absolute introvert who has social anxiety! Presenting is easy for me because no one talks back. Put me in a house party, though, and I have strict strategies (see box below) to follow – that is, if I make it out of my pyjamas and Netflix-filled house!

House Party Strategies for an Introvert

1. Arrive late.
2. Find a pet or child to play with.
3. If there are no children or pets, find a wall.
4. If someone approaches you, resort to social-skill checklist questions:
   a. How is your mother?
   b. What is your favourite food to cook?
   c. Where is your next vacation?
4. Repeat social skills checklist three times.
5. Leave without saying goodbye.
6. Return to house filled with pyjamas and Netflix.

Here is the thing. I hate parties. My close friends know my people capacity is eight, and any more than that makes me sweat. I was fine living in my awkward, introverted way, but then I started to notice something. During every holiday season, we all receive invites for various festivities and ugly-sweater Christmas parties. I was perusing my Facebook invites one day and realized it was mid-December, and *I didn't have any invites!!!* Because of my social distress, people assumed I didn't want to come to these parties. Now, listen, folks. For all of you with introverted friends, just because we hate it, and just because we don't want to go to your social events, does not mean we don't want to be invited!

We do this to kids *all* the time. The most frequent questions I get from teachers when I register students into curricular classes is, "What are *those* students doing there, and what are *they* going to get out of a high-school science class learning about the periodic table of elements?" They assume that just because a student has a developmental disability, being there would be purposeless. Well, my response to that question is simple: What does *anyone* get out of learning the periodic table of elements?

Often, as students with disabilities get older, the fewer opportunities they have to be part of school experiences and learn with their peers (Downing 2008; Willis 2007; Schnellert, Kozak, and Moore 2015). More and more, schools have adopted a self-contained special-education model for students, especially in high school (Downing 2008; Willis 2007). There, students' educational experience is often limited to life skills and functional academics in a segregated classroom (Milsom 2006; Katims 1997; Pugach and Warger 2001). Although I will never advocate for some of these learning activities to be dismantled, I do advocate for balance, because I (and many individuals and parents) don't believe that a program focusing only on functional skills, such as money, time, cooking, and other life skills, is an assumption for any of a student's entirety – including education (Pugach and Warger 2001).

I think sometimes we forget that part of our job in educating our future citizens is exposure. Education has a huge role in exposing students to content and experiences that are not just valued by society but are also interesting. Who knows what students will latch onto in their education journey? I had a student with Down syndrome who was included in a social studies 8 class. During a unit about the Vikings, he developed a huge interest in Viking outfits (the helmet in particular), and for the next five years dressed up as a Viking for Halloween! I will also never forget a presentation I went to where Temple Grandin spoke. For those of you who don't know, Temple is a woman with autism who has revolutionized the cattle industry, designing ethical and humane processing plants for slaughtering cows. When someone asked her, "Temple, why cows? What made you interested in cows?" Her response was perfect, "Well, did anyone maybe think that it's because I was exposed to it?!" (Grandin and Panek 2013)

I have had too many students walk through my door as teenagers whose interests do not match their age. Their motivating activities included watching *Blues Clues, Dora the Explorer,* and *The Wiggles,* and playing on Fisher Price pianos, simply because they hadn't been exposed to anything else. Part of public education is to expose kids to interesting and age-appropriate things. This should not be an exception for any learner (Courtade, Spooner, and Browder 2007).

So what is the goal? What is our vision for education? We cannot just accept individuals segregating to what is safe and/or simply bring together or separate students involuntarily to share space as our goal. It is important to recognize this extension beyond the physical location. If integration is the space, inclusion is the bringing together of students in that space to learn from, and build upon, their strengths and the strengths of others (Kliewer, Biklen, and Petersen 2015).

Building and facilitating community between and within diverse groups is an appreciated method worldwide in education, our workplaces, and our communities (Brownlie and King 2011; Schaps 2003; Gibbs 2006; Senge 1990; Block 1994). Knowing how to work effectively within diverse groupings is a skill that needs to be facilitated, taught, and invested in – just like anything else (Benard 1991; Gibbs 2006). First, though, students – *all* students – need the opportunity to be part of the group.

Inclusion is not about integrating students by housing them into (or out of) forced containers of classrooms and schools. Inclusive education *is* about providing opportunities *with* supports for *all* students to have access to, and contribute to, an education rich in content and experience with their peers. Period.

3

Inclusion Is Not a Place and Time

In the previous chapters, we discussed the differences between inclusion, integration, segregation, and exclusion. We determined one of the key indicators that sets inclusion apart from the other three was the idea of voluntary communities – inclusion needs to be more than people just sharing a physical space.

This definition becomes less clear, however, depending on where in the inclusive journey a classroom or school is. Integration is often the first step in moving these communities forward to be more inclusive. The question that emerges, however, is how to move away from containers of integration and toward communities of inclusion.

If we start by thinking just about the different places or locations that make up a school, we can make a nice detailed list, including classrooms, hallways, theatres, cafeterias, playgrounds, and bathrooms. But now we know filling these spaces with students is not enough, because we know this is integration – student forced together in the same space. So, what makes these places meaningful for students? What makes them a community?

I thought about this while I was doing errands one day after school as I drove to the bank, the gas station, and the grocery store. I realized I went to all these places for very specific purposes. I went to the bank to deposit a cheque, the gas station to get gas, the grocery store to buy my dinner. What became really clear, though, was the places I went to not only depended on the purpose, but also, I didn't go to places with the wrong purpose – for example, I didn't go to the bank to get gas! It sounds obvious and silly, but what if we took this same idea and applied it to classroom contexts? What, for example, is the purpose when students go to math, or phys. ed., or recess? These spaces that kids go to become meaningful once they begin to have purpose. You can imagine, then, how unmeaningful classrooms become when there is no purpose, and it is just a space or a container.

The tricky part, however, is that we often assume kids know the purposes of these different spaces. But if we think about it, how do they know, for example, that it is okay to throw a ball in the gym, but it's not okay to throw books in the library? Or in which classes it is okay to wear a hat or use their cellphone, or when they can talk to their neighbour? I know I am as guilty as any in assuming kids know what is expected of them as they progress through the grades.

We forget these purposes involve skills that need to be taught. What was the first thing we learned when we went to school, for example? We learned how to sit, how to keep our hands to ourselves, and when it was okay to talk! Kindergarten and primary teachers are brilliant at this. They teach kids *how* to go to school, what is expected of them, and then turn those expectations into rhyming songs like, "Hands on your hips, zip up your lips!" or "Crisscross, applesauce!" As students get older, though, we might forget that the same explicit teaching is needed. We replace instruction with, "They should know better," and then pull them out of classes at the first sign of behavioural disruption. What is the purpose we have for our students? What is the vision? And more important, do they know the vision, and were they part of creating it?

If this sounds familiar, it should: this vision of co-existing successfully in a physical place requires positive behaviour supports – anticipating negative behaviours and then teaching the positive skills needed before behaviour goes south (Simonsen and Myers 2015). Having a vision, and teaching students what to do explicitly in different contexts, is a well-documented approach to helping students navigate classrooms and schools (Sailor, Dunlap, Sugai, and Horner 2009). These positive behaviour supports have proven time and time again how powerful such preteaching strategies for behaviour can be (Sailor et al. 2009; Schwartz and Chen 2013).

This physical place is where students can negotiate their different purposes that make placements meaningful. But what are the possible purposes to the various classroom and school contexts? I needed to do some research on this to find out and ended up finding three big themes or purposes that all students negotiate in all the different spaces that occupy their day.

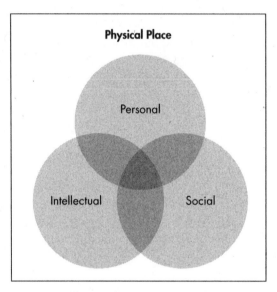

Figure 3.1: Three inclusive purposes.

Within every physical place – whether it is a classroom, the hallway, the land, or a playground – are multiple purposes that individuals can negotiate. The personal, the social, and the intellectual purposes complete a trifecta of establishing how to bring meaning into places by considering purposes within settings (Simonsen and Myers 2015).

Considering each of these themes, we can now zoom in and identify goals to help us define purposes in our classrooms and schools. Personal purposes are goals related to self or goals that enable an individual to exist successfully in a physical space (e.g., behaviour, self-regulated learning, personal awareness, and responsibility) (Kliewer et al. 2015; Butler, Schnellert, and Perry 2015). Social purposes include setting goals involving not only the self in a place, but how the self interacts with and engages with others within a place (e.g., communication, social responsibility, social emotional wellness) (Kliewer et al. 2015; Courtade-Little and Browder 2005). Lastly, the intellectual purpose gives students goals that enable them to have a role in the learning community of a classroom. This community sets the curricular and process goals, including critical and creative thinking, and what students are expected to know and do within their learning contexts. Often, we refer to this as specific subject-area curriculum, but its definition is expanding to include thinking competencies that cross curricular contexts (Downing 2008; Courtade-Little and Browder 2005).

What is important to acknowledge is that these three areas are not compartments and do not stand alone. Every minute, students are negotiating their purposes between these areas.

These areas, or inclusive themes, can help us guide our planning. This proactive rather than reactive process can be helpful, especially for students who or classes that may need additional support in one or more areas. Our role as inclusive educators, then, is to bring "balance to the bubbles," while ensuring students are part of this vision creation. Additionally, these themes can assist us in determining the necessary skills students need to be taught to not only have a role in, but also contribute to, all the places they occupy throughout their day.

An Example: Jack

Jack is a student in grade 7 with a developmental disability who is on a modified program entering high school. It was a priority for him and his family to stay connected to his peers and to be exposed to interesting topics and curriculum. Upon transitioning to his secondary school, Jack, his family, and his grades 7 and 8 teacher teams came together to develop a meaningful plan for his grade 8 entry year. They sat down and discussed interests and strength areas and possible places in the school where he could be meaningfully included. They drafted a list of classes that included phys. ed., humanities, art, and a literacy block to balance his personal, social, and intellectual needs.

(continued on page 22)

(continued from page 21)

Once September arrived, his resource teacher discussed with Jack's other three classroom teachers how these three goal areas could be addressed in each of his classes to ensure he had a meaningful role. They used an inclusion-planning matrix (see figure 3.2) to assist them with their goal development. Jack's Individual Education Plan (IEP) was developed from this brainstorming meeting.

Once the goals were fleshed out, more detailed goals could be decided, for the official plan, but this initial planning document helped organize the team to ensure Jack's plan was balanced and provided him a purpose in every place he was in. The teachers in each of these classes could then use Jack's plan to build the skills he needed into lessons taught to the class as a whole so other students could benefit from these scaffolded supports. The added benefit to Jack's plan was that his educational assistants now knew exactly what the goals were ahead of time and how to support Jack within his different settings.

	PERSONAL GOALS	SOCIAL GOALS	INTELLECTUAL GOALS
Phys Ed	Arrive on time with gym shoes	Ask to join in on an activity	Unit: Basketball – bounce ball consecutively 3 times
Art	Arrive on time	Ask for help when needed	Unit: Watercolour paintings – background and foreground
Humanities	Arrive on time with supplies	Take attendance for class	Unit: World Religions – identify 4 major world religions
Literacy	Arrive on time with supplies	Take turns reading a book with a peer	Unit: Print concepts – identify and use pictures to understand meaning of text

Figure 3.2: Inclusion planning matrix for Jack.

As you can see from Jack's example, addressing the different inclusive goal areas helps to support him having a purpose in every place he is in – like getting gas at a gas station! This idea of balancing purpose is not beneficial just for students with special needs, however (Rose and Meyer 2000; Schnellert, Kozak, and Moore 2015). Curricular reforms are already responding to this idea of the development of core competencies. In British Columbia, for example, the renewed curriculum now includes competencies that all students develop over time, including self-regulation for learning, social responsibility, communication, and critical and creative thinking, to name a few (BC Ministry of Education 2015). These competencies can be developed in any area and nicely align with the three inclusive themes that all students can develop and negotiate between.

Whether it is an art class, an English class, the cafeteria, or the gym, these are the goals students need to successfully be part of their communities – personally, socially, and intellectually. We can no longer assume students know the purposes of all the different places they occupy in a day. This attention to purpose is exactly how we can move from integration to inclusion. Inclusion is not about place and time; it is about place with purpose, and an important step in creating meaningful inclusive settings for all students (Schnellert, Kozak, and Moore 2015).

Inclusion Is Not a Destination

Another one of the myths that contaminates inclusive education is the assumption that inclusive education must take place 100 percent of the time in 100 percent of the places in school – regardless of behavioural challenges, learning needs, and inclusive experiences (Sandall and Schwartz 2008). Now, if I just think about this logically for one minute, I don't even know how it would be possible, even with all the funding in the world. I mean, how many of us go to the washroom with other people (other than to put on makeup and to gossip at parties!)? There are many times in a day when we are not with a cohort or with people of our age and/or ability.

Last summer, I travelled to Denmark for the first time. I grew up in a family that values Danish culture, and my mom, aunt, and uncle did an amazing job of embedding Danish traditions into my life and belief systems. I didn't have a large Danish community to connect with in Alberta, however, so often my only exposure to these traditions was when I spent time with my mom's family – specifically that of her twin sister, JoJo. JoJo and my Uncle Remo have four children, and together, we six cousins, including my brother and me, would come together for family events and immerse ourselves in as much Danish fun as possible. I learned at an early age the importance of taking care of each other, the value of patience, and about the strength in kindness. Uncle Remo, who is also a pastor, would throw hints of the Scandinavian ways into his sermons, and I was always so proud when he included us kids in the stories told to the congregation.

I value these memories, as most people do when they think about their family, but a big part of this was honouring the Danish within us. I had nothing to compare my family to, however, so I just thought the little Danish traditions, decorating styles of my mom, JoJo's delicious baking, and the sensibility and quick wit of my uncle were traits of my quirky and lovable family.

When I was in Denmark, though, for the first time in my life I felt what it means to have a culture. I saw people walk like me; I saw windows decorated as if my mother had made the curtains herself. Everyone ate sandwiches with forks and knives, and in restaurants, I ate off the same style of porcelain that stands in my family's dining-room cabinet. I was so excited when I realized it's not only my aunt who really likes small porcelain figurines; it's that Danish people like small porcelain figurines! It was such an amazing feeling to be part of, and interact with, people who were just like me.

I can imagine there are a lot of students in our schools who feel the same way. Athletes hang out with athletes, and drama kids hang out with drama kids, but somehow other categories of similarities have become stigmatized – and schools have made us feel that if we allow kids to gravitate toward each other out of likeness of ability, culture, race, or language, we need to hide or dismantle these groups for fear of the perception of segregation or exclusion (Laporte 2016).

When working with students who need significant support in learning and other areas of their life, it becomes obvious that time away from their peers might be very beneficial. Some examples could include times for physical or occupational therapy, counselling, toileting support, or to learn and practise explicit skills that will help them in the classroom. Many of these times are needed for kids to maintain integrity, take a break from the noise and movement of a classroom, or even to be with like peers. I can think of many students I have worked with who have benefited from alternate spaces where they are not physically in the same location as all of their peers. Does this mean I am not an inclusive teacher?

World Down Syndrome Day is a celebration attended by individuals with Down syndrome and their families and friends. If you've ever attended one of these days, you know there is nothing segregative about the experience. Imagine the beauty of one person with Down syndrome and then multiply that by 100! Now, this is a party where I do not experience social anxiety. What makes the event inclusive, however, is that individuals are not forced to attend, and it isn't the only community these individuals are part of. At the end of the day, they go back home, or back to their schools, classrooms, and families. In this example, the problem is not that there is a party for people with Down syndrome. The problem that could emerge is if this was the *only* party they got to go to.

The difference between this example, however, and the common arrangements of groupings in schools, is that students are usually corralled by ability and not brought back together to celebrate their diversity and accomplishments. Additionally, these arrangements are rarely offered by choice. In the traditional education model, students are identified and grouped by deficit, and are brought together because they aren't successful, – unlike on Down Syndrome Day, when students are brought together *because* of their strengths and to celebrate each other.

Groups based on deficits are also often passed off to other teachers or support staff to *handle*, with kids shuffled around to alternate locations in schools and given activities rarely aligned with what their home class is doing (Pugach and Warger 2001). If this happens enough times, students move from alternate spaces to alternate programs, and then onto alternate schools.

I went to an alternate program myself, and you know what? I loved it. It met a critical need in my life at the time, but even in my 13-year-old head I remember thinking, "Why can't this just be school? Why did I have to fail to get here?" Alternate spaces are so important in bringing students back up who have fallen. But if the only reason students are finally receiving supports is because they fell in the first place, then we as an education system have to do better. We have to get these supports to kids *before* they fall, in their home communities, schools, and classrooms.

It's also important to remember these traditional pull-out services and alternate settings often benefit *all* kids (Rose and Meyer 2000). For example, many times pull-out will only be arranged for a caseload of students with special needs, as with social-skill groups for students with autism or remediation groups for kids having difficulty with reading or math, regardless of whether other students in the class have a similar need. Many kids, for example, could benefit from the supports and strategies offered to kids with learning disabilities, including hands-on and concrete-based examples, the use of technology, and opportunities to express themselves in multiple ways – this is just good teaching. The same can be said for language support, and in Canada especially, cultural support for our Indigenous students. It is a fine balance, and will look different for every student, classroom, and school. There are debates advocating for both sides of the push-in or pull-out, mainstream, or alternative model of support for students. But if the goal is teaching groups of students inclusively, regardless of whether it occurs in or out of the classroom or school, these supports need to be in place universally, for all kids, regardless of category. Additionally, these supports need to be accessible *before* and not only be accessed *after* a student has been unsuccessful.

When I told my mom I was going on a trip to Europe last summer, she asked these three questions: "Where are you going? What are you going to do there? When are you coming home?" Imagine if we asked these three same questions to students. If a group of students needed some math help, or someone needed speech and language support, or maybe there was a student who needed some counselling support, what if we asked them the same questions: "Where are you going? What are you doing? When are you coming back?" Imagine the ownership students would feel to their home classrooms. Inclusion is not limited by space. Moving between classrooms, hallways, support rooms, the office, and the library are multiple spaces that need not be exclusive to students who need support, either. If all students are negotiating supports inside and outside the traditional classroom space, it is no longer stigmatized as an activity specific to students who have additional needs or are not being successful in one setting.

Classrooms and schools are becoming more and more flexible, and the more we provide choice and share ownership of the success of our students collectively, the more opportunities they will have to be successful in the many places they occupy. The key, however, is that classes are a family, and students belong in their classroom home – whether they are physically together or not. What does it mean to be a family? We know where other family members are, we start together, we end together, and we support each other's strengths along the way.

How do we know when we are being inclusive, then? We need to have common criteria if we are going to address practical inclusion, because it is not always black and white and could be different depending on the class or student. I've worked with a few different school groups, and we have come up with a list of criteria to help us structure activities in our classrooms and schools to meet this goal. This is a helpful checklist for making changes to what we are already doing, which will have big effects on the support and success of all students:

We are inclusive…

- as long as we are always striving to be more inclusive in the classroom, the school, and the community.
- if the goal is to come back and apply the skills we have learned in other settings.
- if we start together and end together as a home classroom.
- if student arrangements are based on goals and not ability.
- if groupings are voluntary and offered as choices to *all* students who need support.

Now, don't get me wrong, I am still advocating for planning and designing learning activities for all students to learn together, but I am also acknowledging that this may happen in more than one physical location. In some of the most inclusive schools, I see kids choosing to work in the hallway, in the library, at desks, or at tables – the more choices the better. Educators are learning that the more ways in which we allow kids to work, the more successful they'll be. It isn't about place. It isn't about time. It is about being purposeful in all places and at all times in a classroom, in a school, and in a community – whether the time we are all together is five or ten minutes a day, a week, or a year! It is going to look different for every student and every class. What is most important, though, is that we never lose the goal of coming back together, to share and learn from each other. The goal does not have to be 100% of the time, but it does mean that 100% of the time we are striving to be more inclusive. It is a journey, not a destination.

Sounds great, right? Now that we all know what inclusive education is philosophically, what about the practicality of making it happen? How do we provide opportunities to students with supports in diverse classrooms? How do we provide meaningful and purposeful placements for all students while maintaining rigour and challenge? Where do we start? These are big questions, and ones I am hopeful the remaining chapters of this book can help answer.

PART 2
What Is Inclusion? Telling the Stories

In Part 2 of this book, you will find stories and examples of how inclusion looks from various perspectives and from people with various abilities, backgrounds, and experiences. Every one of these stories describes how I have come to understand inclusive education, and what it can look like in everyday settings. These practical examples and stories also helped me see that inclusive supports for students who need the most support are often just really clear examples of what all of us need, and I am reminded to never lose sight of the underlying philosophy of why any of this matters. It is the belief that all students belong that drives us forward in our quest to better address diversity. My students and my colleagues remind me of this every day: all students cannot only exist in, but be contributors to, their classrooms, schools, and local communities.

Inclusion Is Presuming Competence: Under the Table

He sat under the table, the pages of the dictionary lightly brushing the side of his left cheek. "He likes math," they told me on my first day. Daniel rocked back and forth, engrossed in his world. Deaf and blind, his residual sight gave him just enough sense – just enough that if he really looked close enough, out of the corner of his right eye, he could determine the shapes of the numbers on the tissue-thin pages. I recognized the repetitive motions of students with autism and the characteristic widespread eyes and faded upper lip of Down syndrome. "How could anyone possibly know that he likes math?" I thought to myself, as I crawled under the table.

"Make them participate, even if it's with their elbow." "Make sure they don't get it wrong." "This is the only way they will achieve success."

Errorless Learning, they called it, and it seemed logical at the time. Under the table I sat, with my flashcards.

"Hey, Daniel, what is 7 + 2? What? Did you say 9?! Great job! How about 10 + 20? 4?! *Yes!* Daniel, you *do* love math!"

And this went on for days, me having a one-way conversation with myself, and Daniel flipping through the dictionary completely ignoring me.

Smack!

His arm flew across my body, the impact in my jaw. In the shock, I didn't know whether to reprimand or celebrate his initiation of contact.

All was forgotten, however, as I looked over with water in my eyes and saw him pointing to the top of the page.

The flash card read 20 + 40. I didn't even have to look at the page before I figured out what he wanted me to see.

The page number in the dictionary read 60. He had been answering the questions the entire time.

In my own ignorance, I had assumed he couldn't do it. He couldn't *possibly* interact with and perform a cognitive function such as mathematical operations. He was too autistic, too deaf, too blind – too disabled.

But, in reality, here I was, the educated specialist, the able, being too unmindful to recognize *I* was the one not communicating with *him*. He had been trying to communicate with me for days.

It wasn't Daniel's ability preventing him from doing math; it was my inability to assess, give feedback to, and communicate with him in his world to see that he could. It made me think – what else does he know?

We assume students don't or can't understand. We talk to them like they aren't there. We think they can't hear or see or communicate. And we are wrong.

Daniel may never fit into the "real" world, but, if I open my eyes and my ears and look at things a bit differently, I might be lucky enough, even if for just a moment, to be in his.

Daniel came out from under the table. We had a common communication base now, one without words, sounds, or pictures, but one of mutual respect and appreciation.

Daniel taught me a big lesson that day, one that has influenced how I interact with every person I meet. He taught me about competence, and he taught me about communication, and most important, he taught me that unless I presume competence in all people, I am the one who is disabled.

6

Inclusion Is Putting People First: A Gay Danish?!

This story is about my mom. Well, not completely, but it starts with her. Before I go further, however, I should tell you a little bit about her.

Imagine a 5 foot 2¾ inch tall, cute, nice 63-year-old with great skin. And now add a homemade, colourful, fluorescent muumuu with matching Crocs and a big smile. My mom (and her twin sister) are *actually* the sweetest creatures that have ever lived. She is always happy, except for these three things that get her mad:

1. She says there is never anything good on television.
2. She thinks there should be a grandfather clause that allows people over 60 to still smoke at the beach.
3. She can no longer buy fabric at Walmart.

My mom.

She loves Lays plain potato chips and the colour blue, buying tables, shopping at the Dollar Store, quilting, and going to the beach. In fact, you will often find her at the beach with a table, wearing the colour blue, eating Lays plain potato chips, and quilting under an umbrella she bought at the Dollar Store.

Mom at the beach.

My mother and I live three blocks apart on Davie Street in Vancouver. She proudly declares herself as "living in the heart of the village," and we will often meet at our neighbourhood coffee local, Melriches, and chitchat about my dog, her sewing projects, and/or her revelations for the week. My mother is very reflective, and often bursts out with profound one-liners. One time, she called me up and left a message on my phone that simply said, "Shelley, *I'm in love!*" only to find out later that she had recently watched a documentary about Leonard Cohen and convinced herself that he was her true soulmate.

One afternoon, as we sat at Melriches, she shared one of her revelations by declaring, not quietly (on Davie Street, I might add), "You know, we could all learn a lot from the gays."

I then made my shocked face. But before I could respond, she continued into a lovely monologue about how happy she was to live in a community that values diversity, and how everyone is different, and that it's okay! And she's right, people *can* learn something from people who are gay, and she *can* walk down the street in her fluorescent muumuus and matching Crocs, and the only people who turn their heads to stare are women (and men) who want to know where they can buy their own muumuu-Croc combo!

She meant absolutely no disrespect to gay people (or to her daughter) by calling us an adjective, so I used this opportunity as a teachable moment.

"So, Ma, you know that *gay* is an adjective, right?"

"What do you mean?"

"Well, I mean you can't call people adjectives when we are people. We are nouns!"

"Oh. Well, that's what I meant."

Now, one more thing you should know is that I inherited a few things from my mother. We are both Danish, we both have cute toes and apple-shaped bodies, and we both manage some mental-health issues.

"I know, Ma, but what if people called you an adjective, like *crazy?*" (which we have both experienced extensively in our lifetime). This one got her.

So, we deconstructed this a bit, and discussed different adjectives we had experienced and compared them with each other. What made some terms okay and not others? Some terms were adjectives. Some were nouns. Some were grammatically correct. Others were not.

And some were mean and should never be spoken.

We used the stem, "If we saw each other walking down the street, what would we say?" as our litmus test. We tried everything!

- Oh, look. There is a gay. (No)
- Oh, look. There is a crazy. (No)
- Oh, look. There is a Danish. (No, I am not a pastry.)
- Oh, look. There is Shelley! (Totally)
- Oh, look. There is Shelley, who is crazy. (Ummm – still no)
- Oh, look. There is the gay Danish! (I don't even know what this means.)
- Oh, look. There is my mom! (Yup)
- Oh, look. There is Danish Shelley. (Sure – at a Viking festival)
- Oh, look. It's BGS (Big Gay Shelley)!!! (Only on Pride Weekend, please and thank-you)

We eventually agreed to just call each other by our names: Ma and Shelley. My mom learned her adjective lesson, and we moved on to the next profound reflection. But, then, I started thinking (and we all know what that means): sleepless nights and multitasking through meetings. Adjectives, labels! We *all* do it. We label and categorize our students all the time, well-meaning or not. Our days as educators are constantly *filled* with words associated with and used to describe kids.

I remember the days when I was a student and the words used to describe me then. I thought about myself as a teacher, a consultant, a speaker, and a person, and the words I use to describe others. I started to make a list, and I added to it for three days. Let me also mention that these words I listed (see figure 6.1) have been heard in a variety of contexts, including in my university class, a special-education conference, a collaboration seminar, IEP meetings, a staff room, the pub, coffee with a parent, and dinner with colleagues, to mention a few. Regardless of setting, person, time, and/or tension, labels and categories were used, and I am just as guilty as anyone.

---

low, modified, bright, illiterate, adapted, gifted, slow, special, low end, waste of space, gay, Deaf, learning disabled, bad, poor, handicapped, queer, good, problematic, core, vulnerable, grey area, crazy, smart, problem, Down syndrome, normal, low and slow, mute, nonreaders, bottom of the barrel, Chinese, drug users, challenged, teacher's pet, high flyers, special-ed, behaviour kids, brown, life-skill, brain damaged, Tier 1/2/3's, resource kids, risk takers, Natives, on the spectrum, Muslim…

And let's not forget the acronyms!!!

A's, H's, G's IEP kids, ELL/ESL kids, SPEDS, and, of course, the ever-present – "Those are *your* kids."

Figure 6.1: The list.

It is a good thing that I didn't hear anyone say the *R* word, because I may have tripped them. I will let you decide which labels were appropriate or not, but I will point out the discrepancy between positive and negative terms. Which labels were you called? Which would you add? I know you remember them – they are not words we forget.

Why do we do this? Why do we need to group people into categories? Is it more effective, efficient, shorter, or easier? Is it what we hear, or all we know? Or maybe we say the words to harm. I have been told that some people use labels because they can't keep up with political correctness and have "given up" trying not to offend others.

But I don't know. Are these good enough reasons? I mean, would you ever see a person on the street and say, "Oh, look, here comes a paraplegic," because it is efficient to say?

No!

Another important question I ask myself all the time is: If I heard that, would I say something? To be honest, I didn't say anything to anyone in my three days of listening.

Why?

We (teachers, people, society) are *so* focused on labels and categories. To be fair, however, I understand that sometimes they are helpful. They can define culture, build pride, and even help bring to the table difficult social-justice issues. The Idle No More movement and the Black Lives Matter campaign are perfect examples of that. And, if we are really being honest, labels and categories are the reason many of us even have a job; categories are how schools get funding to support students with special needs.

Is there a point, however, where in our label obsession, we forget the person we are labelling? And, additionally, how do the labels we place on others affect the people we are labelling? In the book *Choice Words,* author Peter Johnston (2004) reminds us that the language we use creates us and defines the world we live in. The words we use also make a difference to how people see themselves, and how they exist in our world. Words are powerful!

This issue has got me thinking seriously about how I use words in my world. My friend Leyton also reminded me of an excellent point (as he often does). He gently asked me, "How many remarkable people in the world do not fit into *any* category, or into traditional systems and labels? Like you?!"

So, with the help of colleagues, a few articles, and my mom, here are some criteria and guiding ideas to assist you in the use of words (see figure 6.2, page 40).

1. Everyone can read, write, and communicate – expand your definition. Try to argue this with me!! (for example: *nonreaders/writers, nonverbal*)

2. We no longer use these words: *mute, mentally handicapped, illiterate, brain damaged*, the *R* word, or any statement that starts with, "They suffer from...."

3. There are some groups that use labels to define their culture. This is referred to as "identity-first language" (for example: *Deaf, Queer, Danish, Muslim, Canuck*, some people with *Autism*). If this is you, slap a capital letter on the word, put it on a shirt, and wear it with pride, because you were born that way, baby!

4. Say the following labels only if you want to get tripped by me: *bottom of the barrel, low and slow, waste of space,* etc. Just. Don't.

5. *Please!!!* Regardless of adjective or noun – avoid the articles *a, an,* or *the,* followed by label and a period. (for example: *an autistic. a gay. the bright kids. the queer. a gay daughter.*)

6. And lastly, if your choice of words is not something you would say to a student or to a student's mother directly, complete the following procedure:

   a. Write it on a piece of paper.

   b. Stick your gum in it.

   c. Burn it.

   d. Sweep up the ashes.

   e. Put the ashes in a glass of Diet Coke.

   f. Add Mentos mints to the glass.

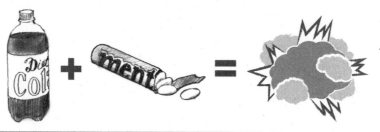

Figure 6.2: Rules of labels used to describe people.

As an alternative, try these:

- There is a movement among some individuals with disabilities, and others working in this community, to use "people-first language" (Folkins 1992; La Forge 1991; Fox 2007), which I encourage everyone to explore and reflect on. It is actually really easy. You do exactly what it says: Use the person first followed by the descriptor (for example, "a student with a disability," "Joan who is Danish," "Shelley who is gay," "a kid who needs support," "a student who has a learning disability," "a teacher who needs a vacation").

- If, by accident, you use person-first language to someone who prefers the capital letter identity-first language (Egan 2012; Sinclair 1999), I *promise* they will be less offended than if you do the opposite. Referring to people first will never be politically incorrect – it's safe.

- If the above option doesn't work for you, you could try just calling them kids, students, or people.

- If the above two options don't work for you, you can always call them Shelley, Kate, Leyton, Carole, Gillian, Faye, or [*insert name here*].

At the end of the day, if you can remember only one thing, remember this: The *only* label we should use before a person's name is *our* (except for my mom, because she is "mine").

And sign the *R* word pledge. So I don't trip you.

7

Inclusion Is Diversity: A Composition

Very often, as teachers, we find ourselves stuck between two historical and political silos: the government vs. the union. I know I am not alone in having experienced teacher strikes many times (and I have an extra stock of Kraft Dinner and hot dogs just in case). One pattern I have noticed in every strike involves the battle between special education and teachers who feel ill equipped to meet the needs of these students in their classes, especially as supports for them diminish. Fair enough.

This struggle is real and is summed up in the media as being about "class size and composition." It makes sense that these issues arise during times of tumultuous bargaining, but I have a really hard time justifying this advocacy for appropriate working conditions, when most other professions in our public-service field are not responsible for advocating for the supports of their clientele. Take doctors, for example; you would never see them fighting for the rights of their patients during their own contract negotiations.

If we put aside funding issues and look at what works, we know there is ample research supporting lowering class size, and I have no argument (nor want to have one) to counter this.

The other word, though, *composition*, is a little more tricky a concept. It is used to represent the ratio in a class of students with special needs to students without special needs. Upon first glance, one may not see the problem. If we look a little harder, though, at the implications of fighting for a ratio of special- to nonspecial-education categorized students, things get a little fuzzy.

To prove their points, teachers and schools have publicly declared their special-education ratios and gone to social media to fill their screen with statistics, describing the horrors of having to teach multiple students with special needs in the same classroom as their "regular" kids. Some school districts are known to even track composition ratios on their websites, so this information is displayed to the public, as if these children are spreading a disease with no cure. I have heard parents say, "Why would you want your child in a class with a special-needs kid, anyway?"

You can imagine the tension I feel when, reading this, I see my colleagues – within a union I am also part of – talking about their class compositions in this ableist way. It would not be tolerated with race – so why is it okay for ability?

For some reason, class composition has become synonymous with impossible teaching arrangements, and reflects a pessimism toward individuals with special needs (Pugach and Warger 2011). Such students are perceived as incapable, and worse, a burden, to other students and teachers in classrooms. Before negotiations, however, the word *composition* did not refer to just ratios of diversity and ability.

In writing and art, the word *composition* means "the plan, placement, or arrangement of the elements of a work." In music, it is "creating and arranging an original piece of music." In the digital world, composition refers to "the practice of digitally piecing together a video" (Wikipedia 2015). All of these have one thing in common – planning and arranging pieces together to create a whole. Did you notice another common theme? In every definition, compositions are *original creations.*

For too long, we have been aiming to teach homogenous groups of students. I guarantee that more than just my music, writing, and digital-composing friends agree "all the same" is undesirable. With these homogenous standards, it is not just students with special needs who don't fit the mould. More and more, students struggle to find success in a paradigm that focuses on deficit rather than on ability.

The educational shift toward inclusion has attempted to counter this attack by embracing diversity and creating classrooms that are not just geared toward the status quo. *This* is what we all should be fighting for – a shift in education to embrace all, not just some. Somehow, though, this value shift has been left for the teachers to carry alone. It is because of this that the concept of inclusion (and composition) has become contaminated with negative connotations, rather than embraced as a philosophy that binds us and brings us together.

My lovely hairdresser, Missy, cut and coloured my hair recently, and in our chair/mirror discussion, she talked about her choir and its sold-out performance this summer. My ears perked up, however, when I heard her casually mention, "We have so many tenors this year."

What didn't follow were these statements:

"The tenor population has increased so drastically because we are so much better at identifying them."

"Ugh, this choir year is *impossible!* These seven tenors are taking up *so* much extra time."

"We found an app that alters a tenor's voice, so we can fit them into our choir now…kind of."

"We needed to compose a whole new piece for them! I don't have time for that, so we found a similar piece they can sing quietly at the same time as everyone else."

"The tenors should probably just be in their own choir. They require a different set of skills that I am not specialized to compose for."

Or my favourite:

"We already have three tenors; sorry."

And you will definitely *never* find a circle graph of current choir composition on choir websites used as a strategic and political scare tactic.

The difficulty with these statements, more than just the obvious "Oh, those poor tenors" is that a composer would *never* say this! Choirs *need* tenors! A choir filled with only sopranos would sound like shrill elevator music on repeat. I love you, sopranos, but I feel like you appreciate the complements of some tenor love as much as I like to turn up the bass in my car when I listen to Beyoncé.

What Missy continued to describe (pay attention to this part) was how the choir responded to having a lot of tenors. This choir commissioned a piece to suit their chorus. In the choir world, a piece is commissioned with the chorus's strengths in mind. So, for example, if a choir has a strong bass section, the piece chosen highlights lower notes. Alternatively, if a soprano section of a choir is smaller, or developing, the piece won't include an extraordinary amount of high notes. In other words, the music is chosen to respond to the *composition* of the group. Missy's choir created an original piece so that the tenors (and everyone in the mix) could feel "included and make a contribution." They didn't make the tenors change their voices, they didn't make them sing a different piece, and they didn't turn them away – those tenors were as much a part of that choir as anyone else. Their presence, however, informed the piece that was created for them. The musical *composition* made the most of the choir's strengths, for the benefit of all. At the end of the day, this choir gave an *amazing* performance (did I mention it was sold out?) And, I bet not one person in the audience knew there was a larger-than-average tenor population. The goal was met. Objective achieved!

Strength-based teaching is not a new phenomenon, and there are many frameworks that can support the spectrums of language, culture, gender, and every other unique identity marker you can imagine – including cognitive ability. These supports are effective in both challenging *and* creating access for everyone (Rose and Meyer 2000).

There are teachers everywhere who are trying to create learning opportunities for all their students *because* of this diversity, not *in spite* of it. This is inclusion. These classroom teachers, however, are having a harder and harder time. There is an obsolete expectation that teachers simply teach to a homogenous group in isolation. How hard can it be, right? There are many difficulties with this longstanding idea, especially in classrooms where teachers are trying to move toward a place of inclusion and access. But inclusion *cannot* happen alone.

The advocacy shifts from changing the composition then, to advocating for supports *for* the composition. If we take a step back and zoom out from the ratio debate and look at this from another angle – a supports angle – we can come up with many ways to support diversity in classrooms (see figure 7.1). You may notice that this list focuses on what can be changed rather than on the characteristics of students, which cannot be changed. Unfortunately, this list is also not regularly seen as necessary, but rather as nice-to-have benefits for teachers and schools.

> › Inclusion needs **time** for collaboration to honour the diverse expertise among teachers and support staff, because we cannot support inclusion alone or in isolation.
>
> › Inclusion needs **funding** to support meaningful curricular goals and plans that acknowledge alternate ways of knowing and understanding the world.
>
> › Inclusion needs **space** for teachers to grow and change their professional practice to respond to the evolving structures of their classes.
>
> › Inclusion needs relevant and diverse **materials** and **resources** to respond to the needs of the diverse students.

Figure 7.1: How to advocate for inclusion.

The supports listed above are not teacher benefits; they comprise a blueprint for inclusive education. Let us not lose track of what we are fighting for. There is a bigger picture to our negotiations framing diversity of ability as a problem rather than as a strength.

There is one more factor for inclusion to be successful. And, I argue, the *most* important one! Inclusion *needs* a diverse composition. Without this, we are simply cookie-cutter assembly-line workers. Without diversity, teachers cannot be the creative composer. This is our career, this is our skill, and we are skill*full* composers.

Let's look to our teachers as composers. Let's consider them the skilled professionals that they are, collaborating together and delicately weaving the diverse abilities, interests, and characteristics of our students into creative, original, and carefully planned arrangements. And let's allow our kids be kids, in their diverse mix, existing in our communities for us to serve, exactly as they are.

Let's stop fighting for class composition ratios, and instead advocate for supporting our compositions in all of their perfect diversity.

Inclusion Is Critical: The Split

In my role as consultant, I ask groups of teachers all the time, "Why inclusion? Why are we doing this? Why are we bending over backwards, spending money, striving to make this happen in our schools? Why? What is the point?"

Answers range from "Because it's the real world" to "Because it's the right thing to do," and they aren't wrong. But they are missing something – something critical.

Here is a story, a story about bowling. Most of us have been bowling. Glowing balls, pins, stinky shoes, garlic fries – bowling.

When we go bowling, we throw the ball down the lane. The goal is to knock down as many pins as we can. We contort our body and limbs into strange positions after we throw the ball, thinking it will help. Sometimes we get gutter balls, and that feels bad, and sometimes we get a strike, and that feels good!

We aim the ball down the middle, at those little arrows painted on the floor, and once we release the ball, all we can do is hope as we peer anxiously down the lane. We listen to the sounds with trembling anticipation, of pins falling, and hope to avoid what usually happens to me when I throw the ball down the middle – the 7–10 split.

The 7–10 split is the most difficult shot in bowling. The split occurs when the only pins left standing are on either side of the lane. Even though we have another ball, the chance of knocking down both pins is rare. In fact, in the last 50 years of televised professional bowling, a 7–10 split (see figure 8.1) has only been hit three times (Grasso and Hartman 2014).

Sometimes, we have great games; sometimes, we have horrible games. If we practise and get coached, we will get better. Bowling, like anything, takes skill. But even after the skill development, coaching, and practice, a perfect game, even for professional bowlers, is very difficult. Most, in the end, will take the safe route and aim for just one pin, knowing very well that in doing so, they are leaving the other one standing.

My question to you, and I encourage you to really think about it, is: how is bowling like teaching?

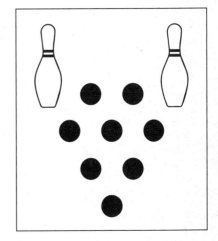

Figure 8.1: The split.

Here are some answers I have collected over time:

- The teacher is the ball, the students are the pins.

- Bowling is loud.

- Sometimes my lessons are a strike!

- Sometimes the ball is so off the mark, I don't even knock down pins in the next lane.

- A perfect lesson is hard to teach.

- Teaching takes skill and practice.

- We get more than one chance.

- We get to wear great shoes.

- One teacher flipped my whole metaphor around and said, "Well. I see the ball as the students, and the pins as teachers." Think about that one!!!

After some discussion, we usually come up with something like: We teach as best we can, and hope to get to as many kids as we can, but the reality is, there are kids left standing who we can't get to, even if we want to, and they are usually the kids who need the most support and the most challenge.

It's kind of a depressing metaphor, actually.

Well, I have another question for those of you who have watched professional bowling. How many times have you seen a professional bowler roll the ball down the middle?

Let me just tell you, if you haven't watched bowling on TV, that there is not one professional bowler who throws the ball down the middle. Professional bowlers throw the ball down the lane with a curve. So, curious as I am, I called up a professional bowler one day and asked him some questions.

"Mr. Professional Bowler," I said. "I have noticed you throw curved balls when you bowl, and I am wondering why."

Mr. Professional Bowler then proceeded to explain, in excellent detail, about the physics of bowling, and the intricacies of the angle of the ball upon pin impact. I will save you the minute details and just tell you that bowlers do not aim down the middle because the ball cannot possibly knock down all the pins by itself: it relies on the other pins to help. So, sending the ball at an angle enables the ball to make initial contact to the most pins. If you think about surface area and the domino effect, the more pins you have contact with initially, the more of a domino effect you create. If you aim for the middle, most often you won't have contact with more than one or two pins. But if you change your trajectory so that the ball enters from the side, more pins are struck, causing a larger domino effect.

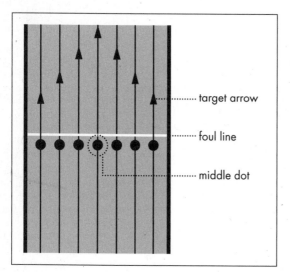

The question I really wanted an answer to, however, was: If you have to curve the ball at an angle to get that spin and trajectory, where do you aim the ball when you throw it?

His answer was the exact answer I was looking for, but the last thing all of us amateur bowlers do. He said he aims for the *outside* pins.

Professional bowlers do not aim for the headpin. They do not aim for the middle. They aim for the pins that are the hardest to hit. You see, the probability of knocking over all the pins is higher if the bowler aims for the outside. The headpin still gets knocked down, but, actually, the outside pins have a bigger role than the headpin in knocking down all the pins. In fact, if those outside pins weren't there, it would be harder to get a strike.

Now – just think about this!

We teach to the students in our classes who have two parents, eat three balanced meals each day, get nine to ten hours of sleep every night, go on family vacations, are involved in extracurricular activities, have limited screen time, have hypoallergenic dogs, and use every colour of gel pen! We teach to the students who need us the least. Why? Why do we teach to the headpins? The headpins will be fine, whether we show up to teach or not.

We teach how *we* were taught. In my case, I went to school during times of streaming and segregation of special-needs students, who were never educated with me. I also asked the professional bowler about this. "Mr. Professional Bowler, hypothetically, would it be more or less difficult if there were no outside pins? What if you just took them away?" His response was perfect, "Well, if you take away the outside pins, you will just be left with a new set of outside pins!" Homogeneity is a myth, and diversity unavoidable.

Classrooms have changed – for the better, I think – but our education system still hasn't. Why aren't we teaching to the kids who are the hardest to reach? Why aren't we looking for the kids who have hoodies over their head and headphones in their ears, who probably didn't sleep much and may be hungry, or even looking to the child who has autism as our starting point – and aim?

We do not need research and formal assessments or observations to know who our outside pins are. You are probably thinking of them right now. What if we changed our trajectories when we plan our lessons and units, if we asked ourselves, "Which of my kids are the hardest to get to? What do I need to do so that *they* get it?" How would your teaching change?

Is inclusion important? Yes, because students have a right to learn. Yes, because learning within diversity is the real world, but, yes, also because these kids, all kids, have contributions to make – whether students have special needs or didn't eat breakfast that morning; whether they are English-language learners, or whether they have a hard time getting to school on time. The students who are the hardest to reach also have so much that we can learn from, too, because if we can get to them, we can get everyone. We often forget that what helps one helps everyone, and it is exactly this idea that makes what we teach strategically more effective and efficient, even in learning communities.

So, I ask you again, why is inclusion important? It is important because we *need* diversity. We *need* each other. We *need* communities of varying ability, culture, experience, knowledge, and language. This symbiosis is important for inclusion to work and be sustained. It is critical, and not just for students with special needs. It is critical for every one of us.

Inclusion Is Learning from Each Other: The "Other" Kids

All I wanted to do was make a bank deposit, but then I saw her look at my name tag. "So, you're a teacher?" Her eyes bolted up toward me from the counter, but somehow, strangely, she kept her head in one position. On a typical day, the above-mentioned question would be one of respect and admiration rather than today's syllable inflection, inferring instead a question and judgment.

Teachers were on strike. In fact, earlier that week I too had been waving at cars, trucks, and bicycles, handing out pamphlets promoting support for "our kids." From about 80 percent of those vehicles driving by us, we were rewarded with supportive waves. But I could tell immediately on this particular day, this particular bank teller was not part of that majority. "So, tell me, what do you think about this inclusion thing?" she asked, as she typed in my bank-card number.

Okay, seriously?! On a slow day at the bank, I would have – what? Three minutes tops of possible conversation time with this person, let alone the hours I would actually need to answer this question with the rationale and justice it deserved.

I had a choice to make. I could say something like, "Uh, well, actually, I do work for the school board, but I'm not a teacher. I'm in payroll," then collect my things and walk away....

or

I could stand with my integrity intact and answer with a deep breath and full sentence, knowing my words could very well be heard, but not listened to. Before I knew it, though, I realized my voice did not matter at that moment, as she continued her thought. "I just, well, I just can't help but wonder what will happen with *my* kids when they get to school. I mean why should my kids suffer because those special-ed kids need extra help all the time? Don't they just hold everyone else back?"

"Ummmm...."

"I mean, what about the *other* kids, the smart ones?"

"Uuuhhhhh...." I was speechless. It was my turn to stare. I could hear the clearing of throats behind me in line, and so I did what any diplomatic strategist would – turned my response into the form of a question. "So, how old are your children now?"

"One and three."

"Well, let's just hope all this strike stuff blows over by then!"

I was relieved I was able to bypass that blow without crying or screaming or pulling out the *Individuals with Disabilities Education Act* conveniently located in the right pocket of my bag. As I walked out of the bank, however, I couldn't help but wonder: Why does she think that? Where do her assumptions come from? What did her life experiences show her that gave her such a narrow perception of ability and diversity?

Then, again, maybe she was a mom who just wanted what she thought was best for her kids. I did, however, know one thing for sure: she neither meant to offend me or my profession, nor my philosophy – she really just believed what she said.

Of course, this snowballed into sleepless nights filled with questions such as, who *else* believes this? Unfortunately for me – many people. This woman marked a moment in my inquirous montage, a moment when the battle set forth before me was confirmed. I am not fighting with people who don't care, or with people whose philosophy differs from my own. I am fighting with people who simply don't know any differently. I am fighting with the history and dynasty of traditional segregative special-education practices predating the memories of people who existed before my time. This is all they know. This is what they believe, because no one has challenged them to think or experience anything differently.

What about the *other* kids, the kids *without* disabilities? Was I the one being naive in truly believing that everyone actually benefited from inclusion?

The following week, I was asked to consult on a case involving a student in grade 4, to discuss assistive technology possibilities for a student whom I had not yet met. All I knew was he had multiple disabilities, was nonverbal, and had little vision. But I also knew as I walked into this meeting that this guy was loved, as his 11-person team of every professional acronym that has ever existed eagerly greeted me.

His name is Ali. He and his family had recently arrived in Canada. Fleeing civil war, they were refugees escaping oppression and discrimination. I was curious about his story. How did he get here?

When I arrived, Ali was asleep. The team was concerned, as usually he was alert and excited. The family's interpreter was asked to call home to check in and make sure everything was okay. As we waited (and Ali snored), a colleague to my right passed me his file.

In respect to privacy, I will limit details, but allow you, the reader, to infer. Ali's disabilities were caused from bullet wounds received in utero. Somehow, though, both Ali and his mother survived. Ali was unable to walk, see, or talk because of his injuries, and without medical services available, his mother strapped this boy to her body and carried him. For five years, she carried him, wrapped tight around her. She carried him out. Out of war. Out of turmoil. Literally heart to heart.

Upon arrival in Canada, Ali was greeted with a wheelchair to carry him now, but for the first year mom followed closely behind his new mechanical form of transportation, metal and cold. I could see colleagues quickly jumping on this: "She can't come to school and follow him around. He needs to learn his independence!"

Ten minutes after the interpreter's phone call, Mom arrived. Ali's back was to the door. In she walked, elegant and modest, in her traditional hijab, and without saying a single word, Ali's eyes opened and his head turned. The interpreter informed us of Ali's predicted trouble sleeping and continued to explain other factors of his lethargy to the team. I, however, tuned out after 10 seconds, as I was enthralled by the interaction unfolding before me.

Ali's mother sat beside him, amid the jargon and professional babble. She put her mouth to his ear and whispered his name over and over, "Ali, Ali, Ali," adding a gentle coo and cluck of her tongue. His lips split to a smile, his hands squeezed hers. His blinking blind eyes turned toward her voice. This was the extent of their "verbal communication," as we practitioners would refer to it.

The connection I had just witnessed between a mother and her child was one that crossed language, ability, time, and place. This connection I had witnessed in two minutes was a deeper connection than I had ever felt in my own 34 years of life. In this situation, I was not the able-bodied.

These two individuals connected on a level not of disability, but on a level everyone in the world strives for. Ali and his mother were the exemplar. They were the able. They were the people whom we seek to understand, whose ability we aspire to.

I could walk down the street right now and find 10 people who would question Ali's life. As a person with such multiple disabilities, what could he possibly offer to this world? How are the costs and resources being used to support him benefiting society? A typical person on the street might assume that these additional costs for special-needs children in education are not recovered (Mayer 2009). I wish I could have videoed this moment of connection between Ali and his mother and shown it to people. I would ask them to watch it and then ask Ali's mother, "Who taught you how to do this, how to connect beyond words?"

Ali's teacher had welcomed him early. She had heard he was arriving and was proactive in contacting additional resources and supports in the district. A general-education teacher with a background in art education, her attitude was not limited, and her philosophy was sound. She came to work with the simple objective of teaching her kids.

With an upcoming unit about adjectives and descriptive words in writing, this teacher spent an evening collecting recycled materials, gadgets, and craft supplies. She piled them on the table and, connecting to the book *That's Not My Dinosaur* by Fiona Watt, designed an activity where every student in the class was to recreate a page of the book. Using the available supplies, students had to use texture to connect to descriptive words. By the end, this class collectively made a book parallel to the published one. This book, however, was filled with rich texture and materials, perfect for any student, but especially perfect for a student with vision impairment. The students worked hard, carefully incorporating mini-lessons co-taught with the district vision resource teacher about contrasting colours and black backgrounds. The learning experience was authentic, rich, and genuine for every student in the room.

Dinosaur book.

Upon completion, Ali sat with his classmates. The book was read out loud, one page at a time. The students watched as Ali interacted with and felt each page made just for him by his peers. He savoured every detail, listening to the words read and turning every page slowly. All eyes locked on Ali, ears open, hands still, all watching and learning. I have been to many classrooms and taught lessons around adjectives, which was far less effective but also boring. Not only was Ali's teacher embedding her lessons in an authentic learning experience, but knowingly or not, this teacher had also aimed her instruction to the student who was the hardest to reach, the outside pin! I had witnessed a perfect example of Universal Design, a framework to support diversity extending well beyond the walls of education and into architecture, medicine, and the world.

Student books.

I would love to bring Ali to the bank. I would love to introduce him to the bank teller as "the boy who taught us." A boy with great purpose in this world. A boy who enriches the lives of his peers, his teachers, his team, and myself. I would show her how we are the lucky ones, as would be her children – children so lucky to be in a class where students of all backgrounds, experiences, and abilities learn from one another.

At the end of the day, and many days beyond, I still catch myself wondering how one of those 14 bullets had not hit something vital to survival. I know for sure that Ali has me reflecting on this and many things, but most of all, he has taught me how we can learn from each other – we all have strengths and we all have stretches, but despite this, we are all, in fact, here. Here to learn, if we choose to reflect beyond what we think we already know about ourselves and, more important, what we think we know about "the other."

10

Inclusion Is Collaborative: The Bears

*Robbie's
Christmas card.*

This is a Christmas card from Robbie, one of my students. When I got it, I took one look at the two bubbly yellow characters with ears right on the top of their head and said, "Wow, those are really nice – bears." He quickly and sharply corrected me, saying, "No, no, no, Ms. Moore, those are people and it's me and it's you can't you tell by their hair look mine is orange and spikey and yours looks like Justin Bieber." Other than the stutter, it was said exactly like this – no pauses, one breath, rocking body. Picture it.

I never made that mistake again. I quickly learned which "bear" was me, and I received seven more of these cards for every year I ever worked with Robbie (and will probably continue to receive). A yellow line on the top of the card, an orange line down the right side, the Robbie and Ms. Moore bears in the top left corner, and its painstakingly consistent message inside, reading, "Dear Ms. Moore, Merry Christmas. I hope you enjoy my card. I like you Ms. Moore. From Robbie." Every. Single. Year.

I should also mention how his lack of muscle tone and fine-motor-skill difficulty prevents him from writing curves, presenting his freehand drawings and written communication to others as an invented cryptic language, consisting of a series of up and down lines and no spaces – which he could totally read.

As sweet as this sounds, the increase of perseveration, resulting from the anxiety developing immediately following Halloween, became overwhelming. The looming deadline would distract him and decrease his learning capacity exponentially, until we finally realized that in November and December, scheduling card-making time during his day would save the sanity of Robbie, his family, and everyone working with him. Even with the added work time at home and school, he had to work harder than any elf in the North Pole to get them done. But as Christmas got closer, he somehow always found a way to recreate these time-consuming handmade Christmas cards for every important person in his life. The structured rules in his brain making sense of the continuum of relationships (by differentiating his family's and friends' cards, respectfully substituting the closing "I love you" for the former with "I like you" for the latter), these cards could easily number in the 50s. Robbie is a popular guy!

I tell you this story not to describe how and why it could be difficult to work with Robbie, but more to give you an idea of what his brain is like, restricted by the boundaries he has been forced to create, to cope in what many refer to as "the real world." Robbie's secondary symptoms, common to individuals who have Prader-Willi syndrome, involve obsessive-compulsive tendencies that trap him (and his family) into routines that most of us will neither experience nor understand. I admire his structure, routine, and ability to manage his life within a giant universe of inconsistencies and the forever-changing rules and expectations placed on him to fit into the real world by typical and able-bodied people. From my (and many others') perspective, he has done phenomenally well.

I am sure one can imagine what Robbie's Individual Education Plan (IEP) would look like. Traditional, category-specific goals around self-advocacy, awareness of disability, and self-regulation followed him for all the years of his schooling – which is valuable, don't get me wrong. But they meant little to teachers who were teaching him art, science, or anything outside of the resource room.

A few years ago, Robbie brought me his report card. It was a piece of paper sporting the school's symbol and motto, listing his name, his courses, and the number of times he was late and/or absent. On his course list, which on a typical report card housed percentages and letter grades communicating a student's progress, Robbie's course progress markings included (and were limited to) asterisks, a perfect 100 percent, a single line that stated "see comments attached," or the most common, a blank.

Comments were rarely attached to the back of his report card, let alone any description of Robbie's performance or progress in any course, or of any content expectations outside of resource room and traditional special-educational programming. Progress was arbitrarily limited to comments such as, "He'll get something out of it." But no one (including myself) really had any idea what that "it" was.

For a school (and district) that prided itself on inclusion of exceptional students, this infuriated me. After my initial freak-out ("What is wrong with you people?!?!?!"), I realized it wasn't that teachers didn't want to assess these kids or give them a meaningful report card, but that they had no idea how.

The goals on Robbie's (and other students') Individual Education Plan had little or nothing to do with the content of the courses they were in. In secondary schools, it's common to juggle 30-plus students (special education or otherwise) in seven or eight blocks, which quickly adds up to responsibility for up to 240. Attempting to provide them all with meaningful programming that fulfills their grade and course-level performance standards understandably leaves the tracking and reporting of toileting routines a low priority.

What is also not taken into consideration is the fact that 99 percent of these teachers may have only received the single required special-education survey course taken by teachers in university, which simply extends their pedagogy of special education to DSM IV[1] labels and diagnoses. Differentiation strategies (at least when I attended) included in the lesson plans created by my fellow future teaching leaders were simply stated in a single line at the bottom: "I'll pair them up with the bright kids."

Although pre-teacher training in post-secondary institutions is getting significantly better in preparing educators to respond to and plan for classes of diverse students, including those with high-incidence disabilities (learning disabilities, English as a Second Language, behaviour, reading and writing difficulties, and so on), teachers are still not provided sufficient background knowledge on how to differentiate, adapt, and modify content for students with the most significant needs, including autism, Down syndrome, and multiple disabilities such as deaf-blindness. Although inclusion is encouraged in schools today, these students' "inclusive" experiences with teachers are limited to greetings and attendance before being pulled out, for a few minutes, for phys. ed., and (if an amazingly supportive teacher is found) minor participation in elective classes (home ec., art, woodworking, and so on). The content-area teachers simply do not have the expertise to make these contexts inclusively meaningful.

This is a great time to acknowledge the incredible educational assistants (EAs) who make *any* of this possible. If these students *are* given the opportunity to attend a class with their peers, it is the EAs who are often the ones doing goal-less modifications and adaptions on the fly to help students participate as meaningfully as possible, whether such roles and responsibilities are in their contract or not.

To begin to tackle the integration (a.k.a. no purpose in settings) issue in our school, I went on a hunt for a teacher. I had a student, I had an EA; now, I needed a teacher who was willing to spend some time with us to create some purposeful goals specific to particular content area. And where did I go? Straight to the art room! I didn't have the necessary diagnostic assessment that could clarify specific goals Robbie needed in art simply because they don't exist, but I *did* have – the Christmas card. It

---

1   Diagnostic and Statistical Manual of Mental Disorders, 4th Edition

was a great piece of evidence that could be used as a baseline performance-based assessment to help determine some art-related goals. I reviewed the Christmas cards, and made a list of art goals.

Possible Art Goals for Robbie

1. Consider an audience when writing (i.e., type messages instead of writing).
2. Use a colour photocopier to decrease the amount of time, and mass produce the parts of the cards that are the same.
3. Photocopy templates in which he can insert information easily.
4. Take and use photos of him with the person the card is directed to.

All of the art-goal ideas, I thought, would help ease Robbie's anxiety and perhaps help him enjoy the pre-Christmas excitement that occurs in the four weeks before the holiday break.

As I overconfidently brought my list of ideas to the art teacher, I was all ready to review them and see how we could incorporate them into her program, thinking this would be a great way to provide a direction for Robbie's inclusive program in art. I am wondering right now if you, the reader, can see where this is going. Clearly, I *did not.*

Within one minute, the art teacher looked at the Christmas card and said, "Oh! Well, he needs to work on filling up white space, using a variety of shades and colours, and on background and foreground." There you have it. We now had goals, and none of them were mine. What I had failed to realize was that although my intention was to include him meaningfully in this art class, I missed the entire purpose of my quest: none of my goals were content related.

This was the moment I realized the value of collaboration. Although, as his case manager, I knew inside and out the innermost workings of Robbie's goals and development related to his special-education category, I was neither an art expert nor did I have the background knowledge and lens through which to view Robbie's Christmas card to determine the art-related goals he needed.

I could easily have been deflated, but rather I was thrilled. I got it! I *needed* these teachers, just as much as they needed me. I did not, in fact, know everything. And the best part, I didn't *need* to know everything. We cannot do this alone. Collectively, however, we have the experience, knowledge, and expertise to teach and support every single student in our school, district, and community.

After this simple three-minute conversation, we (not I) were able to draft up an art-specific Individual Education Plan we later coined a "one-page content area IEP," which was content-specific and provided a guide for Robbie, the teacher, and the educational assistant. With a purpose for the activities, everyone now knew what to focus on, while Robbie participated in and completed the assignments alongside his peers.

A perfect example of inquiry, this concept snowballed, and we started to compile together one-page content IEPs that are modified for students and included in secondary classes. The amount of time in classes, work output, and student independence increased exponentially. The EAs loved it, and the teachers started to get involved.

These IEPs became relevant, the teachers became invested, and these simplified content goals started to become the universally designed and enduring understandings that everyone in the class could benefit from.

In my seven-year tenure, our school went from 0 percent to 100 percent teacher participation in goal development, implementation, and/or assessment of students with developmental disabilities included in their secondary content classes. The one-page IEP listed the goals, and eventually evolved to include a rubric to assess student progress. Parents started to receive report cards that read "see comments attached," and there would be not only a comment, but a rich description of activities, progress, and now an entire new set of data to help determine goals for the following year.

This became our department's mission, to continue to develop the goals to make inclusion of these students meaningful, starting first with electives and eventually moving onto academic subjects. It is a sustainable concept, still going strong, three years post my departure. There is nothing more satisfying than seeing the torch being passed and continued, brilliantly I will add, by my successor and former team members.

The farm.

So – did it work? Did Robbie learn? Did he achieve his individually set goals for art class? Well, I will leave you with this – a picture submitted to the school's annual silent art-auction fundraiser. A perfect summative assessment and piece of evidence used to communicate to his parents when report-card time came around that Robbie did, indeed, exceed expectations. Filling up white space, using a variety of colour, considering background and foreground. Check. Check. Check.

Despite the fact that I had to fork out 325 well-deserved dollars to get this piece of art to hang in my office, it is a great example of the effects of collaboration and the simple belief that everyone can learn. More important, however, it was Robbie's own way of telling me that there is absolutely nothing about his cards that needs to be changed, for I am one of at least 50 proud people who, every year, await our cherished Robbie's bear Christmas card.

11

Inclusion Is Multiple and Diverse Perspectives: My Bully

SNAPSHOT: *1. an isolated observation, 2. to photograph quickly,*
3. a brief appraisal.

I hate snapshots, and the snapshots I hate the most are school photos. I grew up in the days when cameras were expensive, and even if you had a camera, you had to wait for your film to be developed – if you remembered to bring in (or not lose) the roll. If you also came from a poor family like mine, there were definitely no cameras to be found, which put *a lot* of pressure on the *one* school photo that was taken every year. *One.* That's it. *One* photo to represent you as a person for an *entire* year! Can you even imagine? These days I take one photo every 30 seconds just of my dog!

Now, this one photo was very high stakes. This photo was sent to every friend and family member, was hung on their walls, carried in their wallets, or set on their pianos for everyone to talk about and ogle. This would be fine *if* the one photo was a *good* photo. Unfortunately for me, however, my school photos rarely made the cut for okay, let alone good, so I can just imagine the conversations around my photo on the piano.

Let's take my preschool photo, for example:

Preschool.

Can you guess which one is me? Of course, I am the one pouting in the bottom-right corner, probably because I didn't get to hold the sign. Back in those days there was no running to look at the camera screen to see if it was good or not – this was it. On seeing it, my grandparents probably immediately called my mother, asked why I was such an angry child, and told her she should be more firm, or something.

And then there is my kindergarten photo (see page 68). You may be asking yourself: Why is Shelley smiling like that, and why is her dress so tight? If you didn't know the story behind this photo, and this was the *only* photo you saw of me for an *entire* year, you may wonder many *other* things, like, "I wonder if she has been assessed," or, "Maybe her teeth are rotting because her

Kindergarten.

Grade 2.

mother lets her eat too much candy," or even, "Hmm. She's a little pudgy for a five-year-old, don't you think?"

Well, from *my* perspective, there are actually very reasonable explanations for this photo. For example, I wore this dress when I was a flower girl for my aunt's wedding. My mom made this dress and I *loved* it, and I just *had* to wear it for photos! The problem, though, was that I was a flower girl when I was three. As a very strong-willed child, my mom learned quickly to choose her battles, and willingly safety-pinned the back closed and sent me on my way.

As if that wasn't enough, I also received my first lesson in sarcasm that year. I'll never forget lining up for photos and my teacher telling us, "Now, remember boys and girls, don't show your teeth!" Everyone else seemed to get the memo that this was a big joke, except me, of course, who couldn't figure out (a) how to smile and not show teeth and (b) why anyone would want to smile without showing their teeth.

Grade 2! Not bad. I actually *like* this photo – this year was okay! I can't think of anything horrible about this photo besides the few fly-aways. The problem wasn't this year, however. The problem was the next year, when apparently I forgot what I wore the year before, because I put on the *exact* same outfit *and* thought it was a great idea to trim my own bangs. Imagine the phone calls my mother got that year. "Joan, do you need some money for clothes for Shelley?" And we probably did, but that wasn't the point!

Grade 3.

Grade 5.

Grade 6.

Okay, here we go. Grade 5. The mullet. It was a full-on party-in-the-back, business-in the-front mullet, although I liked the variety in poses.

Unfortunately for me, the severe zoom-out in grade 5 did not help the full zoom-in on the year I got chubby, wearing a pea-soup-coloured turtleneck. When put beside each other, I actually look like I had turned into marshmallow.

Ahhhhh, grade 7. This is when things started getting interesting. Even though I experimented with a perm in a box, I was feeling good! I felt ready for my big year in junior high! I look happy, confident, and ready for anything! Unfortunately, this snapshot isn't very accurate, either. Grade 7 was actually the worst year of my life, and you can tell, because I went from looking like Tigger to Eeyore. *No one* got sent my grade 8 photo (see page 70). In fact, until now, this photo had not been seen by anyone, including my mother. This is what unhappy teenager Shelley Moore looked like.

Grade 7.

Grade 8.

Onto high school! Life is better. I was just too busy, however, to remember things like photo day, and I'm pretty sure I'm wearing pajamas in all of these photos.

It was in high school that I also started to realize that I was less girlie than the others and thought accessorizing would help. If you look closely, you may notice my variety of jewellery – hemp-braided cat necklaces and the seven earrings I thought would be a good idea. Oh, and the hair wrap – let us not forget the hair wrap.

Grade 10.

Grade 11.

Grade 12.

I made it! Grade 12, although no one would have known. This photo is only a proof. That is because I didn't even order this photo – mostly because I tried unsuccessfully to look like a girl and thought ringlets and lipstick were a great idea, until I found some terrifyingly similarities to a Little Bo Peep costume at the San Francisco store.

I bet you can absolutely imagine the glory I felt when I could afford to buy my first camera and experience the joy of immediate editing! Let us all just take a moment to appreciate the advancement of technology for the sake of awkward children all over the world.

Now, I realize I am taking a big chance sending these gems into the world to be scrutinized – and this is exactly my point. Why

Grad.

do we do that? Photography may have evolved, but many things still haven't. How many times a day do we see or interact with people and jump to conclusions, make assumptions or judgments, and react when we only know one story, a single snapshot of a moment, a brief appraisal? How would our world change if we instead started looking for more than one perspective to a snapshot or more than one story to explain an event? How many times, for example, have we muttered under our breath and judged the parent of a toddler having a temper tantrum in the grocery store? As the mother looks on horrified, we have to step over him as we grab the Kraft Dinner and run – out of embarrassment for her. Maybe we have a bit more patience if we have been that mom before, or even that kid. But what about those of us who haven't? We see it all the time: you only have to read the comments on YouTube for 10 seconds to see profanity, criticism, judgments, and assumptions being thrown around beneath the veil of virtual anonymity. Why do we do this? Why do we feel the need to share our story at the expense of others because we think or assume that it is what is right?

We have *all* been the little screaming kid in the grocery store. Maybe he is hungry, maybe it's past his naptime, maybe he stubbed his toe, or maybe he just really wants candy?! Who knows? That is exactly the point: no one *does* know.

How would our perception of things change if we stopped assuming and reacting, and instead, started looking for, asking, or connecting to more stories to help us understand?

Here is a story, a single snapshot in time. Picture a primary-school desk with the chair neatly pushed in. A pair of red shoes sits on top. You may be thinking it's the end of the day, or week, but definitely nothing extraordinary, just a typical day. We see this snapshot all the time. This is one story.

What if I told you this was your class? How would you respond?

But here is another story. Those red shoes were my shoes, and they were brand new! On the Friday I left them on my desk, it was an ordinary day. That weekend, however, my mom, brother, and I left my father. In the night, we packed up what we could carry and moved to a new home, to a new neighbourhood, to a new school.

Fortunately, for me, I remember *nothing* of this traumatic event. Unfortunately, for me, however, I do remember the trauma of knowing I wouldn't be going back to the classroom where my brand-new red shoes were! I remember crying and being *so* upset about those shoes. I *loved* those shoes. This was a big deal to my five-year-old self!

Does your perception change now that you know another story?

Here is yet another story. What I didn't know that weekend, when I was grieving the loss of my red shoes, was that my teacher, who taught kindergarten in the morning at my old school, also taught it in the afternoon at my new school! What I didn't know that weekend while I was melting down about red shoes as my mother was trying to rebuild our life was my teacher brought my red shoes *to my new school for me!* So, on Monday afternoon, when I walked into my new classroom to start my new life, there were my red shoes, sitting on top of my desk, with the chair neatly pushed in.

This is *the* story, and I have not forgotten it 30 years later.

Here is another snapshot.

Meet Kid A. Kid A is a "behaviour" kid. Kid A starts a fight in a phys. ed. class. Kid A beats up Kid B. Kid A gets suspended. Kid A is recommended to attend another school that better meets her needs. This is one story.

What if I told you that Kid A is registered in *your* class? How would you respond?

But here is another story. Kid A was me. And this was my grade 7 year (remember the worst year of my life?). I was bullied, I got fatter, my family got poorer, and my mom got sicker. I refused to go to school; I hid in the church across the street, and the church ladies fed me grilled cheese sandwiches. I failed every class. I hated all my teachers. I felt invisible. I felt alone. And Kid B was my bully.

How does your perception change now that you know another story?

This is also the year I was sent to an alternate school, and this was the year I met Mrs. Smith. In a year of turmoil at school and life, Mrs. Smith was my teacher, my parent, my friend, and my home. She didn't read my file, she read me, and she knew exactly what I needed – and none of it was in the curriculum. My two years in that school continue to affect me to this day. Where Mrs. Smith caught my heart, Mr. Leppard caught my brain. For the

first time in my life, I felt smart, like I could contribute to this world. There was one more teacher I had that year, whose effect I didn't realize until much later. Leyton Schnellert taught me that year, too, and he is the one who I would describe as the teacher who caught my life. If there were cracks I was falling through, it was directly because of these three people that I didn't. This is *the* story.

I asked Mrs. Smith years later, "Why did you care?" Her answer: "Shelley, I knew what you had. I didn't know what you didn't."

I have never forgotten that, 23 years later.

Snapshots tell one story. But what if we looked at another snapshot from another perspective? What are the other stories? The stories we can't always see? The stories we might have to search for and ask questions about before we can really understand what is happening?

This is inclusion. This is diversity. To be inclusive is to collect stories, and be the detective seeking to understand the full story. The more stories we have, the more we understand. Whether it's ability, culture, experience, language, or knowledge, we all have lenses to see through, and we all have a story to tell.

So, next time you see a student crying or acting out, a parent avoiding phone calls, a pair of shoes on a desk, or two kids fighting, I urge you to ask yourself: What are all the perspectives, and how are you going to collect them so you understand the story?

...

My story used to end there, a nicely wrapped-up finale describing the importance of perspectives and diverse lenses. But then something happened.

Here is another story. Remember Kid B? The bully? Well, not too long ago my bully contacted me. Twenty-two years after our fight in the gym, a message on Facebook popped up on my screen. It asked how I knew my bully, and I responded with two words:

my nemesis.

For 22 years, I had harboured so much hatred for bullies. I held a zero-tolerance policy in schools and the community. I didn't care if you were a kid, a parent, or a woman in the dog park – if you were a bully, I would actually growl under my breath. My mantra went something like this: *Look out bullies!!! There is no place for you here!*

Her response? "Nemesis? I'm hurt. Was it really that bad?"

> **...nemesis??**
> nemesis ... i'm hurt ... what it really that bad??
> (was)
>
> **Shelley Moore**
> yes.

My response was simple: "Yes." Of course, accompanying my *yes* was a 12 000-word essay about all the horrible ways she had ruined my grade 7 life!

Now, I'm not sure if you notice what I was clearly failing to realize at the time, but I was absolutely reacting and not following my feel-good, get-to-know-the-full-story protocol. I did, however, start to notice something funny in her response to my life-ruining monologue, which read:

Shelley, what are you talking about? We never went to Jr. High together. We lost touch after grade 6 and rarely ever saw each other.

What?! This did not fit my script – the script so carefully manifested in my head for 22 years. Did I make it up? How could she *not* remember what was so clear in my head?! And then I kept reading:

I honestly don't recall a lot of my youth and now looking back I am regretful of so many actions.

...my first step-dad was an alcoholic...I went through many situations that scarred me for a very long time.

...I moved away from home before my 16th birthday.

...I never even finished high school.

I still hold many hurtful memories (much like you)...

I will never forget reading the words written to me that day. She was so honest, so vulnerable, and so true. This person was not the monster I had created and been carrying around in my head. This person was struggling and blocking out trauma and all of a sudden sounded like someone very familiar; she sounded just like me. How could this be the same person?!

The closing of her email got me right in the gut: *My memories of you and I are happy ones…it deeply hurts me to know you hold different memories of our times.*

I read the last of her words and finally realized – I was doing to her exactly what I was preaching to others not to. I was judging, assuming, and reacting to *one* story without any interest in pursuing, connecting, listening, or looking for *the* story. I was guilty of my own crime, and all I could do was cry when it hit me: I was her red shoes.

Before grade 7, my bully and I were best friends. Inseparable! We went to daycare together, we were in the same class, we played violin, and I practically lived at her house! We both loved putting coloured ropes in our hair, the weird alien Alf, Hulk Hogan, and the Mini Pops. To this day, I still remember her phone number. I don't even know my *mother's* phone number!

She was my first best friend.

My bully is no longer my bully, a label slapped on her unfairly, out of judgment, assumption, and grief. She is now and will forever be referred to as my first best friend – my first best friend who, like me, dealt with trauma and struggled through life's unfair circumstances at too young an age. I have a new snapshot now – nope, I have many – because I no longer have just one story. I have a new one. I have hers, and together we filled in the gaps in each other's story.

My first best friend taught me about perspective; she taught me about the importance of stories. And she taught me that if we only have one story, we will never know what is real. This is *the* story, and I won't forget it – ever.

12

Inclusion Is Leaving No One Behind: The Sweeper Van

There is a concept in architecture known as Universal Design. It is a framework that extends far beyond architecture and into education, medicine, technology, and mechanics (Rose and Meyer 2000). To understand it, we often use the wheelchair-ramp metaphor. When a building is retrofitted to add a ramp for users in wheelchairs after it's been designed and built, the cost is much higher than if the ramp was incorporated into the building's design to begin with. We see this all the time, and today we wouldn't find a newly built building without these accessibility features. This concept has rolled over into many areas of life, including curb ramps, and universal features of computers, such as voiceover and magnification. Apple's Siri has made features like a reader and scribe available to everyone, rather than as extra and often costly added programs. Even the car industry has made a universal move to include back-up cameras and parallel-parking features for cars.

The key to understanding the concept of backward design, however, is not just that supports are being designed and made more accessible for people from the start, but that anyone can use them. The wheelchair ramp in buildings, for example, although designed for people with mobility problems, does not display a sign that says, "Wheelchairs Only." We have all used ramps, regardless of our mobility, as do people with baby strollers, kids on skateboards or bikes, and even dogs, little kids, or big kids who have a hard time with stairs.

Although supports are made available to students in schools, part of this universal phenomenon hasn't transferred as well. Supports in schools are still considered "cheating" or are limited to those who have to *prove* they need them, often through very expensive and high-stakes testing. Only then do students receive the benefits and supports that would otherwise be considered an accessory to our everyday lives.

We still hold a traditional view of education, where kids are expected to learn alone, without supports, in a competitive, race-like environment of conformity. If a student doesn't fit, this deficit model has typically sent kids to other settings to receive supports and get "fixed," and their fellow students don't have access to them. You can see then why inclusion, a concept that values diversity, would be difficult to achieve in such an environment.

I remember learning about Universal Design as a framework in university. Like many things in university, I thought I understood it. But I didn't really get it until I was able to experience it firsthand.

In 2009, I was working at a high school as a resource special-education teacher. This school was known for its amazing Christmas parties. In fact, we had so much fun at these Christmas parties that we had to find a new location each year because we weren't invited back to the previous one.

Every year we would have different activities, but one activity every year was the trick 50/50. The trick 50/50 was a raffle where, if you win you have to give half the money back, because it is a fundraiser for a charitable organization. If you don't give it back, you look kind of like an ass.

Anyway, the 50/50 for this particular year was for an organization raising money for cancer research, involving teams of people riding their bikes from Vancouver to Seattle. If you have ever done it, you will know that you should probably just skip the ride and give them your money – it is really hard! But, of course, I didn't know that yet.

Once upon a time, I did a triathlon. You know – the run, bike, and swim. The bike was the easiest part. So, in 2009, five years later, it was announced at the Christmas party, "We are looking for volunteers for our team!" I was like, "Oh, so easy. No problem. I'm in! I've got a fast bike. I have tights. I can do it."

On our team of nine, we each committed to raising $2000, and the team members went on training rides…*they* went on training rides. While I gave excuses, including but not limited to, "You know what? I'm busy. I'm doing my PhD, and I just don't have time. Plus, the bike is the easiest. I'll be fine. I'll take lots of breaks. Whatever!"

For six months my team trained – without me – while I polished my bike.

So, the day comes in June. It was early morning. I had my fast road bike, all polished and ready. My tights on, my helmet strapped, my bag filled with juice boxes – I was ready to go!

And, actually, if you have ever done the ride, it's amazing. There are thousands of riders, and everyone is wearing yellow, and if you were a cancer survivor, you had a yellow flag on your bike, and you could see these flags everywhere. It was amazing and inspirational.

So, off we went, all thousands of us.

Ten minutes in, I thought, "Hmmm, I wonder if Seattle is downhill?" After an hour, I realized I needed a new strategy because pedalling was no longer an option – my legs already felt like Jell-o! So, I came up with a new strategy, to spend some extra time at the pit stops, eating an extra sandwich, making some friends – I mean this wasn't a race, right? What was the rush? Until, of course, the pit stops started running out of food and closing before I got there.

This was only day one! And this was a two-day ride! It was hundreds of kilometres! I was starting to get worried….

So, as I was riding my bike, there was absolutely no one around. A guy on a unicycle passed me, a pregnant woman passed me, a seven-year-old on training wheels passed me, and now my pride was getting a little tarnished, and I was starting to think this was a really bad idea.

There was no cellphone coverage; there were no friends. It was just me and the cows of rural Washington. I had completely given up on hills at this point. I couldn't even call my mom! And then – it started to rain. I couldn't be saved, and there came a moment, where in the depth of my despair, I surrendered, sat on the ground, and prepared myself to spend the night on the side of the road.

It was a sad moment.

Finally, after sitting and pouting for a while, a van pulled up and the driver asked, "Hey, you wanna ride?" I had two responses to this question: (a) heck yes, and (b) stranger danger. Before I could answer he said, "Actually, that isn't a request. You have to come with me. I am the sweeper van."

After I thanked the heavens, I dropped my bike for the driver to deal with, I got into the van, saw a pillow, grabbed it, and in my exhaustion, fell asleep in five seconds! I don't even remember him closing the door! And this was just day one!

While I was fast asleep, the sweeper van drove me to camp. This was a two-day ride, and so halfway through, we stopped for the night. Dinner was made and our tents were set up. I reunited with my team, as we watched and listened to inspirational speeches from survivors and parents of kids who have gone through the toughest situations. We were back to feeling revved up again, even me, and inspired. I went to sleep with a renewed perspective: "I can do this, I can do this, I can do this…."

The next morning, I got on my bike ready to grab the day by the horns! I took one stride and thought, "I can't do this!"

I don't know if you have ever gotten on your bike after not riding it for five years, but it isn't your legs that are sore! All I kept imagining was putting a cold raw steak on my bike seat.

But now I knew – there was a sweeper van! So I rode my bike, looking over my shoulder for hours! Because I knew it was coming, though the day felt like it was 35 hours long! But I was *not* going to give up this time! I was going to do this. Even if I had to go slow, even if I had to walk, even if I had to crawl – I was not quitting!

Well, the sweeper van came, and after sighing and telling myself, "Well, Shelley, you did the best you could," Mr. Sweeper Van rolled down his window and shouted, "Hey, there! I thought I might run into you today!"

I got into the van, thankful and relieved that this two-day torture session was almost over. Mr. Sweeper Van and I, well, we start chatting. "Tell me, Shelley, why did you do this?" he asked.

"That is a *really* good question," I said. "I'm not exactly sure – maybe because I think I'm invincible and forget that I'm 35 and that my body can't do what it used to. But to be completely honest, I feel really embarrassed. I think I even regret signing up for this. I just, I should have trained. I should have worked harder."

And with a good ear, he just listened to my reflective rant about how disappointed I was in myself. I mean, people did this race who are cancer survivors! I totally took advantage of my health and body. After a while, he finally said, "Hey, I brought you something!" And in his cooler was an ice-cold beer.

It was perfect. It was exactly what I needed!

We sat for a while in silence, as I waited eagerly to arrive at camp so I could enjoy my beverage. But then, all of a sudden, he stopped the van and said, "Okay, get out!"

"What?! Why?! What did I do?!" I said.

"Shelley, the finish line is just through those trees. Go on, go finish!"

"What?! No way! I can't do that, that's cheating!" I exclaimed.

"Why is that cheating?" Mr. Sweeper Van asked. "What is the goal of this bike ride? It sure isn't a race! It is to raise money for cancer research, and to experience something emotionally and physically difficult, and to push your boundaries – all of which are goals I can definitely attest to you achieving! But, Shelley, what is most important is you experienced something amazing with a group of people who all shared a common goal. Why shouldn't you cross the finish line?!"

Stunned, I got back on my bike for the last kilometre. Sure enough, the finish line was right through the trees. I rode my bike across the finish line. Everyone cheered for me! I held my bike above my head for the photo! No one even knew I had ridden in a van most of the way!

Now, let's just think about this. Look at all the supports I had in place that day.

The sweeper van. The sweeper van, which was available for whoever needed it. It was there to make sure no one was left behind on the road – thank goodness! But that sweeper van was not there for me. That sweeper van was for the pregnant woman riding her bike in case she went into labour! But that wasn't enough for me that day. I also needed a nap. But that pillow was also not for me, it was to elevate someone's leg in case it was broken or something!

But even that wasn't enough for me that day. I also needed an ice-cold beer (okay, maybe that *was* meant for me).

When I was riding my bike across the finish line, I realized: This is Universal Design! None of those supports were designed for me. I am healthy, I am able-bodied, I have a bike that works, and I have aerodynamic spandex! The idea, however, was that although the supports were in place for specific reasons and groups of people who might need them on the day of the ride, *anyone* who needed them got access to them. No one said to me, "Oh! You didn't train. Well then, you have to sleep on the road. It's your fault, you should have tried harder," or even, "If you get in this van, you are cheating."

What is most important here is to think about what our actual goals were. The goal of this ride was not competition or that I had to do it alone or that I had to be the fastest. And none of these goals are the goals of education, either. What are the goals of education? The goal I want for students is to look at how we can all do our best, teachers and students alike. How can we know and use what supports will help us along the way, so that everyone can cross the finish line?

An administrator I once had, Kathy Champion, said to me, "Shelley, can you imagine if this was how school was? Where kids, right from kindergarten, knew that if they needed support it was okay – they didn't have to learn alone; they would never be left behind? If they looked over their shoulders, they always knew a sweeper van was coming? Our kids in high school would be a completely different set of people. Imagine the confidence they would have!"

Every day, every unit, every lesson, should have a sweeper van. And although these supports may be designed for specific groups or categories of learners, when the time comes to actually learn, whoever needs those supports gets access to them. Because sometimes kids are tired, and sometimes kids are hungry, and those supports can help everyone cross the finish line. Support is critical, and if we want inclusion to work, this is one of the biggest changes we can make in our classrooms and schools. Supports designed for a few, but available for all.

Now, there is one more part to this story. One of the members of our group of nine riders that day was our administrator, Lorne Bodin.

Within a year of this bike ride, Lorne got cancer and passed away. Our school broke. It actually shattered into a million pieces. Because every student, teacher, parent, and staff member knew if anyone believed all kids should cross the finish line, it was Lorne.

Going through this bike-riding experience, despite the blood, sweat, and tears, became even more important, because it was the last thing Lorne and I did together. It became a goal I didn't even know I was meeting. I will treasure those two days in my heart so closely.

Lorne Bodin.

So, you never actually know the interactions and meaning that will occur when you bring people together and support them to get there. Because things happen, like riding with Lorne, and we don't even know it is important until six months down the road. It isn't about curriculum, or assessment, or grades, or tests. It is about a connection I had with one of the greatest administrators, teachers, mentors, and friends I have known. I learned so much from him, and would have missed out on that key learning if I hadn't received supports that day, which enabled me to experience this event with him.

If I leave you with one thing, it is this: When you see students in your class, do not look at them as a category. Look at them as people who may need support. Think about supports in layers that are designed for specific students, but that everyone has access to. Students do not need to go down the hall to another class or to another teacher to get supports. They can get what they need right there, because there will be another five kids who may also need supports. Look to these students as the guide for others whom we sometimes miss when identifying needs. Think about the power in creating the supports and access for *all* students to be successful. That way, they can all cross the finish line together and meet goals they may not even know are meaningful until 10 years down the road. Leaving no one behind, this is Universal Design for learning.

Acknowledgments

Ten years ago, I couldn't have imagined this book would be an option for me, let alone a reality. Struggling through school, I remember the day when I realized it wasn't me that had difficulty; it was the schools I was attending that had difficulty teaching me. I will forever be thankful for the teachers who did see me, despite the box I wasn't fitting into, developed my stretches, and helped me discover my strengths so I could shine. It is because of them that I am here. I mention many individuals through these chapters, some friends, family, colleagues, and students. Allow me to acknowledge these individuals for teaching and guiding me through this journey, regardless of their age, gender, culture, experience, or cognitive ability.

I want to first and foremost acknowledge the land for which I work, and the amazing Indigenous communities that have welcomed me with open arms to learn alongside and collaborate with. My mom and my sidekick, Finley. My family, including JoJo and Uncle Remo, my brother, David, and his wife, Kayla; my cousins Jens, Anne, Paul, Sara, and their partners and growing families. My teachers and friends Leyton Schnellert, Shannon Smith, and Stephen Leppard. My students Robbie (and his incredible family), Daniel, Ali, Justin, Brian, Troy, and the many others I wish I could mention! My friends Danica Fidler, Kate Campbell, Wendy Arnett, Annabel Duncan-Webb, Jennifer Riddel, Jill Lange, Jill Crockett, Trevor Corneil, Nata Belcham, Patti Parker, Allison Henning, Jordo, Missy Clarkson (and Cor Flammae), Jaimee Charlie, Roseanne Gallichio, Nisha Edichandy,

Karen Hamdon, the Jensen/Pedersen clan, the Riddels, the Duncan-Webbs, the Langes, and everyone who still invites me to Christmas parties, even if I don't show up. My colleagues and mentors Faye Brownlie, Deborah Butler, Sarah Loat, Barbara Bradford, Kathyrn D'Angelo, Kathy Champion, Carole Fullerton, Linda Watson, Nicole Widdess, Cindy Miller, Maureen Dockendorf, Judith King, Vicki Rothstein, and everyone on BCTELA. To the individuals in school districts, schools, and classrooms who have invited me to their beautiful communities, made me cookies, taken me on wine tours, bought me sunflower seeds and my favourite coffee creamer. Who have booked my hotels, flights, cars, and have given me hunting advice! To the organizations that have supported my learning outside of the box, Mary Butterworth Junior High, Simon Fraser University, and the University of British Columbia. A special mention to all the students and staff at McNair Secondary and PS 63, and a *big* thank you to the Richmond School District and the District Support Team, who have fully embraced the knowledge that you can't change the wind in me, but have used the wind to my fullest potential. And lastly, to all the people who listen to my stories, who laugh, clap, and cry all at the right times, and who support the vision of diversity and inclusion in their own life, and in their own way, every day.

Oh, and, of course, the sweeper van driver.

References

American Psychiatric Association. 2000. *Diagnostic and statistical manual of mental disorders,* 4th ed., text rev. Washington, DC: Author.

British Columbia Ministry of Education. 2015. *Draft curriculum.* https://curriculum.gov.bc.ca

Benard, B. 1991. *Fostering resiliency in kids: Protective factors in the family, school, and community.* Portland, OR: Western Center for Drug-Free Schools and Communities.

Biklen, D. P., 1985. Mainstreaming: From compliance to quality. *Journal of Learning Disabilities* 181: 58–61.

Biklen, Douglas, and Jamie Burke. 2006. Presuming competence. *Equity & Excellence in Education* 39.2: 166–175. Web.

Block, M.E. 1994. Why all students with disabilities should be included in regular physical education. *Palaestra* 103: 17–24.

Brownlie, Faye, and Judith King. 2011. *Learning in safe schools.* Markham, ON: Pembroke.

Butler, D. L., L. Schnellert, and N. E. Perry. 2015. *Developing self-regulated learners.* Don Mills, ON: Pearson.

Composition. 2015. Wikipedia. https://en.wikipedia.org/wiki/Composition

Courtade, G., F. Spooner, and D. Browder. 2007. A review of studies with students with significant cognitive disabilities that link to science standards. *Research and Practice for Persons with Severe Disabilities* 32: 43–49.

Courtade-Little, G., and D. Browder. 2005. *Aligning IEPs to academic standards for students with moderate and severe disabilities.* Verona, WI: Attainment Company.

Downing, J. E. 2008. *Including students with severe and multiple disabilities in typical classrooms: Practical strategies for teachers,* 3rd ed. Baltimore, MD: Brookes Publishing.

Downing, J. E. 2005. Inclusive education for high school students with severe intellectual disabilities: Supporting communication. *Augmentative and Alternative Communication* 21: 132–148.

Egan, Lisa. 2012. I'm not a "person with a disability": I'm a disabled person. www.xojane.com